Praise for
JESUS IS BETTER THAN YOU IMAGINED

"Jonathan paints a picture of a God who loves a good surprise and meets us in ways we may not have considered. So read this book expectantly. It will shatter your misconceptions and help you encounter a God more wonderful than you ever conceived."
—Mark Batterson, *New York Times*
bestselling author of *The Circle Maker*

"With his usual word-magic, Jonathan Merritt reminds us that Jesus has survived all the embarrassing things that we Christians have done in His name. He shows you the Jesus who challenges the chosen, includes the excluded, assaults closed minds, opens hard hearts, and defies all the boxes, categories, and camps... the One who left the comfort of heaven to join the struggle on earth to show us who God is and what love looks like with skin on. It is an invitation to fall in love—maybe again, or maybe for the first time—with love-made-flesh, and He's better than you could ever imagine."
—Shane Claiborne, activist and bestselling
author of *The Irresistible Revolution* and
Becoming the Answer to Our Prayers

"Jonathan speaks to the human heart, with words poured from his own. This book is one of the bravest works I've had the privilege to read. May his strength inspire ours."
—Rebekah Lyons, author of *Freefall to Fly*
and cofounder of Q Ideas

"Theology divorced from autobiography is like making love out of a love manual. With JESUS IS BETTER THAN YOU IMAGINED, Jonathan Merritt gives us a theological gem based on his own life story. This book got me so excited about Jesus that it almost left me winded. If you have ever despaired of the church, or departed from the faith, or know someone who has, there is no better book on the market to illuminate the darkness with lightning strikes of divine presence and power."

—Leonard Sweet, bestselling author, professor (Drew University/George Fox University), and chief contributor to Sermons.com

"Jonathan Merritt is fast becoming one of the most influential Christian writers today. He has a pulse on culture and a gift for communicating. JESUS IS BETTER THAN YOU IMAGINED is a practical and poetic book that leads readers into the arms of a sometimes startling God. In a time when young people are growing disenchanted with religion, this book comes not a moment too soon to remind us that Jesus is all we need."

—Brad Lomenick, president of Catalyst and author of *The Catalyst Leader*

"Jonathan Merritt is an incisive, winsome writer and one of the best storytellers I know. In JESUS IS BETTER THAN YOU IMAGINED, he invites us to move beyond legalism, beyond cynicism, and beyond fear to the feet of Jesus, where love always prevails. This book is both brutally honest and stubbornly hopeful. Grace permeates every page."

—Rachel Held Evans, *New York Times* bestselling author of *A Year of Biblical Womanhood* and *Evolving in Monkey Town*

"Well-written, bold, and honest...this book by my friend Jonathan will no doubt introduce many seekers, skeptics, strugglers, and 'saints' to the Jesus they've never known but longed to meet—One who gives grace to broken and burned-out people without disclaimers, qualifications, or asterisks. A true celebration of one-way love."

—Tullian Tchividjian, pastor of Coral Ridge Presbyterian Church and author of *One Way Love: Inexhaustible Grace for an Exhausted World*

"True to the genre of the younger evangelical leader memoirs, there is an honesty and an integrity in Jonathan Merritt's JESUS IS BETTER THAN YOU IMAGINED. But what drives Jonathan's story is a recurring emptiness on the part of a believer who probes spiritual disciplines, creation, struggles with sin, and ultimately God in the face of Jesus. That probing overshadowed everything in this book for me, a probing I found both honest and encouraging, a probing that does not pretend doubt and dryness are gone once one is a Christian. Jonathan's story will be encouraging to young and old alike."

—Scot McKnight, author and New Testament professor at Northern Baptist Theological Seminary

"Candid, blunt, honest, exciting. Jonathan Merritt opens the window of his private life and lets us look and listen in. He tells secrets most of us don't talk about. Sometimes painfully hard. Sometimes exhilarating. Sometimes disappointing. Always pushing toward Jesus, who exceeds expectations."

—Leith Anderson, president of the National Association of Evangelicals

"Stirring, soaring, surprising. This is a delightful glimpse into the epic greatness of the Lord Jesus Christ."

—Frank Viola, author of *God's Favorite Place on Earth*, *Jesus Manifesto*, and *Epic Jesus*

"This honest, raw, emotional, and insightful work from Jonathan Merritt will have you seeking—and finding—God in both the expected and the unexpected. JESUS IS BETTER THAN YOU IMAGINED sheds light on how God works in both the chaos and the mundane of life. Throughout the book, Jonathan continually shows that no matter what you are going through in life, Jesus really is better than you can ever imagine."

—Thom S. Rainer, president and CEO of LifeWay Christian Resources

JESUS *is*
BETTER
THAN YOU IMAGINED

JONATHAN MERRITT

Foreword by
JOHN ORTBERG

New York   Boston   Nashville

FaithWords
Hachette Book Group
237 Park Avenue
New York, NY 10017

www.faithwords.com

Printed in the United States of America

RRD-C

First Edition: April 2014

10   9   8   7   6   5   4   3   2

FaithWords is a division of Hachette Book Group, Inc.
The FaithWords name and logo are trademarks of Hachette Book Group, Inc.

The Hachette Speakers Bureau provides a wide range of authors for speaking events. To find out more, go to www.hachettespeakersbureau.com or call (866) 376-6591.

The publisher is not responsible for websites (or their content) that are not owned by the publisher.

Library of Congress Cataloging-in-Publication Data

Merritt, Jonathan.
    Jesus is better than you imagined / Jonathan Merritt ; foreword by John Ortberg. — First Edition.
        pages cm
    Includes bibliographical references.
    ISBN 978-1-4555-2787-8 (hardcover) — ISBN 978-1-4555-2788-5 (ebook)
    1. Spirituality—Christianity.   2. Jesus Christ.   I. Title.
    BV4501.3.M4827 2014
    248.4—dc23

2013038683

To Margaret Feinberg,
whose commitment to the craft of writing
and passionate pursuit of Christ inspires me

Contents

Foreword

There is an ache that I recognize because it mirrors one of my own.

"This is how things are."

Violent despair in Haiti. Deep sadness in a child. Harsh judgment among the pious.

"This is how things are."

When someone names how things are, when someone tries honestly and in love to help define reality, something in the heart is healed. I don't understand why, but it's part of how the heart works.

Jonathan Merritt has a gift for naming how things are. To do this well involves an art more delicate than surgery, identifying what does not belong and ought to be removed while still leaving in place all that is healthy and needed for life. It requires a refusal to pretend. And this Jonathan does with a combination of courage and love.

Every human being thinks about God. A friend of mine says that all human beings think about God more than about any person, whether we recognize it or not. Those of us who think about Him over time, or are brought up to do it, or do it professionally, face certain challenges. We can say so many words about God that after a while we're not sure exactly what the words mean anymore.

In a class I once took on psychopathology (a class no pastor should leave school without taking), Arch Hart made a fascinating observation about religion and a personality test called the MMPI. The MMPI has a scale designed particularly to detect false answers. Research indicates that religious people tend to give more false answers than nonreligious people, and the more conservative their religion, the more false answers they tend to give. The reason this is so, Arch suggested, is that those of us inside a strong faith tradition tend to confuse our aspirations with our achievements.

I thought about that tendency as I read *Jesus Is Better Than You Imagined*. Jonathan writes about receiving a Master of Divinity, which he says is "a misnomer if there ever was one." I have one of those, but through either naiveté or hubris was never struck by the incongruity. It's a form of compartmentalizing, I suppose. I can say I believe all kinds of things until one day when I bump into reality and find out I don't.

This is how things are. But that is not the whole story. There is also, to borrow a phrase from Neal Plantinga's wonderful book on sin, a way things are supposed to be. And it is there, somehow, at the intersection of how things are and the way things are supposed to be, that we find Jesus. In Him, the darkness of the former does its worst, and in Him, the beauty of the latter shines most fair.

It is *this* Jesus, the real Jesus—with all His confusing majesty in the midst of the real world with all its confusing pain—who shows up on page after page of Jonathan's book. We see Him in the silence of the desert and the beauty of a storm, in the challenge of an impossible assignment and the euphoria of an answered prayer. And not just there. We see Him, through this book, in somebody's life. Jonathan's integrity and thoughtfulness and courage and vulnerability will be a salve to every reader. We meet Jonathan, as we meet Jesus, at the foot of the cross.

Jonathan is a child of the church who speaks without the subcultural accent that so often keeps those of us who speak "church" from sounding fully human, or perhaps from *being* fully human. In his writing we are reminded above all that Jesus is *real*, that He cannot be bound by either formulas or expectations, that He pops up in the most unexpected places because He is actually choosing how He will interact with His world and books His gigs without an agent.

There are many reasons to read this wonderful book. It is beautifully written. It will introduce you to a wonderful voice. It contains much wisdom. But the best reason to read it is for the One who lurks within. You will meet Him at how things are, and He will take you to the way things are supposed to be.

John Ortberg,
Senior Pastor of Menlo Park Presbyterian Church
Author of *Who Is This Man?*

JESUS *is*
BETTER
THAN YOU IMAGINED

0

Holy Expectation

They say that God is everywhere, and yet we always think of Him as somewhat of a recluse.

—EMILY DICKINSON

remember the day the emptiness came. The church service had just concluded, and volunteers were beginning to clean. I sat alone in the worship center, hands trembling. That place within my soul once filled with passion for God was now a foreclosed home with only traces of the family that once lived therein, full of vacant rooms where the echo of one's voice could be heard. The God who had once seemed to breathe on my neck was now a ghost in the distance, blurry and noiseless. And His church, a place of respite for me nearly all my life, was a painful reminder of the absence I felt.

In many ways, my journey to the church had been a long one. And yet, I had nearly always been there. Born Jonathan Michael Merritt at 6:02 p.m. at Baptist Hospital East in Saint Matthews, Kentucky, I met the world with expectation. My mother says I came out with a tuft of hair—wet, blackish locks that rested atop my round face—and crying. Months later, the hair fell out but the crying remained. Riddled with colic, I sobbed perpetually. My wails rose with the sun awakening the morning, broken on occasion by short naps. Even in infancy, I seemed to pine for something more, something just beyond my reach.

Nine days after my birth, I attended church for the first time. I'm told that I was the main attraction in the nursery: the pastor's newest son, pink-faced and barely a week old. An esteemed member of Buck Grove Baptist Church before I could even pronounce the name.

Dad would soon accept a pastorate in Laurel, Mississippi, and when I was three, in Snellville, Georgia. For the next eighteen years, I'd spend countless hours at First Baptist Church, a place that would shape my early view of who God was and what the apostle Paul called "the body of Christ."[1]

The God I met there was a decent chap, so long as you didn't make Him mad. He tended to be rigid and temperamental. I knew of a few of His tantrums, even once transforming a woman into a salt pillar for disobeying Him. When I read Jonathan Edwards's sermon "Sinners in the Hands of an Angry God" later in life, it barely induced a yawn. That's exactly how I pictured the Almighty.

My God was incapable of chuckling at mistakes, grinning when I bumbled down the wrong path, or overlooking my misguided attempts to live the "good life." Instead, the God I believed in peered over my shoulder, shaking His head and whispering, "Go ahead, but you'll pay for it."

To keep my God happy, I aimed to live according to a list of dos and don'ts. This fit squarely with the way I read the Bible—like most children raised in conservative evangelicalism—as a rule book that told me which bad things to avoid and which good things to do daily or hourly or perhaps more frequently.

The don't list was far more extensive than I can enumerate here, ranging from the prohibition against tattoos, earrings, and long hair to a strict boycott of "demonic" television shows like *The Smurfs*, *The Simpsons*, and *Teenage Mutant Ninja Turtles*. I made sure not to drink, smoke, or curse (at least where anyone could hear me), and I stayed far away from any movies stamped with a capital *R* in a thin white box. At restaurants, I cast disapproving stares at patrons who ordered a glass of wine or a foggy beer. "If only they knew the Lord," I'd say to myself, clicking my tongue. I avoided every item on the don't list with Talmudic devotion, feeling I was somehow earning God's favor with every painful sacrifice.

During my preadolescent years, I'd stare into the darkness from my bed late at night, squinting to think of anything I may have done wrong that day. *Did a lustful thought weasel its way into my mind? Did I vent unrighteous anger at one of my brothers? Did I disobey my parents' wishes and thereby dishonor them?* As infringements inevitably came to mind, I'd confess them out loud to God. And I'd always end by asking Him to come into my heart and save me. Just in case it didn't stick the night before.

The to-do list was far simpler. It basically included evangelism and church attendance. Sharing one's faith was critical. After all, I had a moral obligation to do as much for God as possible before He came back to rescue the chosen few and obliterate everyone else. So I had to work hard and quickly. I prayed before meals in public and carried my Bible to school. Though never mentioned in the Scriptures, these were logical actions taken by true disciples who weren't ashamed of their faith.

On Tuesday nights, we'd visit homes in the community to drop off religious literature. On Saturdays, I'd often load into a van with other kids in my youth group early in the morning to "knock on doors," which is Christianese for waking people up before they wished so we could argue them into a "right relationship with God." Sometimes our guerrilla tactics worked, other times not. But every slammed door was a badge of courage pinned on a martyr's lapel. Over lunch, we'd often brag to one another about enduring the rudeness of those we visited, never once considering we might be the obnoxious ones for showing up unannounced at eight in the morning.

When I wasn't pounding on strangers' doors, I was sitting in a church pew—the other big item on my to-do list. Sunday mornings. Sunday evenings. Tuesday nights. Wednesday nights. And pretty much any other time when there was special programming. This was essential to staying on the Almighty's good side. Devoted church attendees like myself would often lament the "Sunday-morning Christians" who only appeared once per week. These individuals were probably going to make it to heaven, we surmised, but they were destined for a less-than-pleasant judgment day when God would wag His finger at their lukewarm commitment to the delight of the rest of us who'd made the extra effort.

Most days, I loved going to church. Everyone felt like family, from the young women with their toddlers to the old men with their hallelujahs. The ubiquity of gaudy brass decor and burgundy carpet made you feel like you were someplace important.

Other days, church felt like pure drudgery. A predeath purgatory. Waking when all I wanted to do was sleep in or stay home and play. Those days church was like walking on hot coals—the only benefit was relief when it was over. Regardless of my disposition, I knew I needed to be there because church was where God lived, and I wanted to know Him. The church was the exclusive watering hole for the spiritually parched.

My views found confirmation in what I observed around me. Everyone at church was perfected by it. Or so I thought. They smiled a lot—that good ol' "joy of the Lord," I suppose—and seemed to live holy lives. I was shocked later in life to discover that many of my childhood friends' parents divorced as a result of hidden alcoholism or affairs or mental illnesses.

During my twelfth year of life, I began to realize that though I had been practicing Christianity, I'd not fallen in love with Jesus. At five, I had walked down the aisle of our Baptist church as the choir beckoned me with a refrain of "Just as I Am." An usher met me at the front pew, and I informed him that I needed to be "saved." I didn't want to burn in hell for eternity. Does anyone? Staring down my teenage years, however, I stood at a critical crossroads.

As I wrestled with the decision about which faith to follow, I underwent a time of what a Christian might call "spiritual warfare" and an atheist might call "hallucinations." Regardless, my Baptist upbringing gave me no framework for processing these experiences. I'd feel the presence of demons when alone, sensing dark presences in the corners of my room while I attempted to drift off to sleep. One evening, Mom prepared dinner in the kitchen while I watched television in the living room. Lying on the floor with my head propped on a couch pillow, I caught a glimpse of a face in the window next to me. It was neither monsterlike nor beautiful. I ran to the kitchen like a bolt, never sharing the occurrence with anyone but afraid to be alone.

Both good and evil seemed to be observing my internal struggle, waiting to see which path I'd choose. Late one night, just shy of my thirteenth birthday, I rose after midnight and sprinted to my parents' bedroom. I grabbed my father's arm and shook him.

"Dad, wake up. I know you think I became a Christian many years ago, but I didn't. I've made up my mind now. I want to follow Jesus."

Wiping the crusties from his eyes and willing himself awake, Dad led me back to my room by the hand, and we knelt together by my bed. I prayed to God, telling Him that I was ready to make an irrevocable decision to follow Him until I drew my last breath on earth.

A warmth crept from my toes through my bent knees to the crown of my head. My breathing relaxed, and I felt the most wonderful peace, as if the Divine was wrapping His eternal arms around my shoulders. Dad kissed my forehead before he returned to his bed. And I never saw or felt a dark presence again.

The next morning I began searching for that warmth of God again, and the place I figured my journey should begin was the location where I believed He was most readily available: church. And every so often I found Him there. When I descended beneath the water's surface at baptism, I sensed a shimmer of heat. I'd hear the gospel in a new way during a sermon and feel the temperature rise. And yet I never sensed that same God presence from my conversion night.

In college, I became something of a spiritual vagabond, roaming from church to church hunting for the Divine. I strained to grasp Him, but God was always inches from my fingertips.

After graduation, I sensed a call to serve God vocationally, and seminary seemed the most logical place to start. I decided to root myself in parish work. Packing up my childhood belongings the night before departure, I felt a bit like Abram and Sarai. I did not know exactly where this journey would take me, but I trusted that God would be my travel companion. Sustaining me. Guiding me. I'd have to walk by faith and not by sight, an easy cliché to share with others but a difficult one to embrace in this moment of uncertainty.

The first day of classes was an exercise in frustration. Everyone around me seemed to know God intimately. Even completely. They had formulated answers for life's most difficult questions. And their callings were so much clearer than mine. Fellow students hadn't just been called to serve God vocationally, they'd received a heavenly letter directing them to become a church planter in West Africa or a youth minister in their hometown. I wondered, why hadn't God called me with the same specificity? Maybe they had learned to listen better.

The next season of life was spent back at my home church, this time with an office, a part-time position, and a second diploma framed on my wall. The embossed document declared, "Master of Divinity." A misnomer if there ever was one. Who can master the unmasterable? Who can claim to have figured out the incomprehensible? Not me.

My time of service was a period of sweet struggle. Crafting sermons, trying to make much of Jesus. Calling people to faith and reminding those who found it to keep doing justice, loving mercy, and walking humbly with God. I came to love those I ministered to, and I wanted more than anything to lead them into a rich relationship with God.

But the love and investment was rarely reciprocated at the same level. Church seemed a magnet that attracted Christian hitchhikers, thumbing a ride to pass through whatever difficulty or New Year's resolution they currently faced. And as soon as they pushed through the other side, they'd quietly eye the off-ramp and ask to pull over.

Gone.

Some, gone for good.

Rather than trust these souls to God, I took it personally. They *must* have left because I did something wrong. Perhaps I should have taught more captivating lessons or phoned them more often. Every absent chair became a challenge to work harder. I tried to balance my increasing workload with budding writing opportunities, a juggling act that often left both efforts unfinished. I was moving bricks from one stack to another. Worse still, I was moving further away from the God I wanted so badly to draw near to.

Ministry had become a job. Another waypoint in my efforts to save the world. I spent more time talking *about* God than talking *to* Him. More time describing God's presence than bathing in it. I had become a travel agent pointing to God like a far-off tourist attraction when I should have been traveling there myself.

In the sixth chapter of II Samuel, King David of Israel dances wildly in the streets of Jerusalem. He's building his kingdom's capital there and has decided to bring the Ark of the Covenant as a symbol of God's blessings and providence and presence. When he realizes the weight of the moment, David is overcome with emotion and is swept up in the sacred dance of worship.

As this dramatic scene unfolds, the storyteller reveals a watcher—Michal, the daughter of Saul and David's wife. She's peering out a window at David's brazen praise—he's stripped down to his skivvies now—and growing angrier with each gyration of her husband-king. David returns home to find Michal has seethed to an overboil. In a shoutfest dripping with sarcasm and insults, she attempts to shame him.

In the midst of this great worship service celebrating God's blessings on His people of Israel, Michal never lifts her hand, never sings a note, never whispers a grateful prayer. But why?

For one thing, Michal is mired in the past. She's bitter that her father's dynasty was traded for David's. The Scripture describes her as "the daughter of Saul" rather than "David's wife." Michal is angry because of what God did or didn't do in her life, what other people did or didn't do. And she can't move beyond those disappointments.

Worse, Michal had become an observer rather than a participant in the dance of worship. And I had become Michal. Like Jesus's first disciples,[2] I was battling cardiosclerosis. My heart was hardened, clogged by the traditions of religion and the cardboard God I had created. As a result, church attendance became a feast on a stale cracker: dry and unfulfilling.

I craved more.

That's when the emptiness came. With the worship center lights dimmed and only a few remaining voices echoing in from the foyer, I sat down to contemplate the impasse I'd reached. I couldn't give up on God, and yet I didn't want to continue my current spiritual path. This would mean embracing an unbearable future, one where I engaged God out of duty. We'd become an old married couple, sitting on the couch with each other each evening, rarely speaking. Sure, we'd stay together, but I'd always wonder if I'd hung around longer than I should.

God, I want to stay with you, but I can't keep doing this.

I looked down at the Bible resting in my lap—leather splitting at the edges, color fading. This seemed a metaphor for the state of my spirit, but perhaps it also held the answer to my question. I thought about the wild and wondrous God encounters I'd learned about in childhood through songs and Sunday school, from walking with Adam and Eve in a garden to the ethereal visions of John the Revelator.

The God I met in the Bible loves surprises. He makes a habit of showing up in unexpected ways and at unpredictable times. God comes in floating ax heads and talking donkeys, in water from desert rocks and flaming bushes that never burn up. He causes the sun to shine for an extra day, and parts seas like a bad hairdo. In thunderstorms and on silent nights, God comes when and where people aren't looking. Even the birth of Christ underscores God's love for surprise. While the rest of the Jewish nation was looking for a kingly figure reminiscent of David, God sprints toward a manger in a peasant town. God comes in the form of a wandering Aramean, a nomad Nazarene.

What's more, God rarely shows up the same way twice. Sometimes He meets people in the wilderness and other times in the city. Once He even met a runaway preacher in a fish's belly. He shouts at Samuel, but whispers to Elijah. He speaks audibly to Abraham and Isaac, but when Joseph takes the stage, God seems to catch laryngitis. He comes to Joseph in dreams instead. The same God who meets Daniel in visions meets David in the wise words of an honest friend. Why? He may have been trying to keep them on their toes.

Suddenly, my eyes widened, and I sat straight up.

Perhaps my frustration wasn't stemming from God's absence in my life. Maybe He was there, but I wasn't looking for Him. The God of the Bible is not one who settles in a single place waiting for us to show up, but one who scatters His presence in every nook and cranny like wedding rice.

When Jacob was on the road to Haran, he witnessed the great ladder connecting heaven to earth that touches down in the strangest of places. "Surely the Lord is in this place—and I did not know it!" he exclaims after waking from his dream. Jacob responds by building an altar and calling the place Bethel, or "house of God." The lesson is clear: God is not confined to temples and synagogues and churches. His house has no walls and no door.

My mind flooded with questions:

Was I walking through life with eyes glazed over like the star of a zombie thriller, unaware of the Holy in my midst?

Is it possible that the God who created me is better than the God I've created?

Could it be that the true God—that Jesus—is better than I imagined?

I was tired of the mundane business of professional Christianity, weary of leaning on bumper-sticker-sized half-truths—sometimes when God closes a door He *doesn't* open a window—and ready to abandon a Christianity that colors inside the lines, ready to encounter this unexpected God.

The magi who visited Christ's birth flashed into my mind. The way they departed the comfort of their homes with no marked-out destination. They had stars in their eyes and a sense that maybe something spectacular—maybe God—waited in the dark distance. We don't know their names or how many wise men there were, but we know that when it came time to leave, they "went home by another way." Not the route marked out on their maps or the way with which they were familiar. They forged a new path home and God was walking with them—a God who looked different than He did on the trip's first leg.

I thought of Pentecost and the band of doubting disciples huddled together around mere memories of their executed master. They were discussing what to do next, as if anyone knew, and then it happened. A wind swept through the room, they breathed it into their lungs, and when it came out again, it made words they did not know they knew. Sparks like struck flint flashed above their heads and made flames, and the commotion was so loud that people rushed from every corner of the neighborhood to see what was causing it. After a while, the uproar died down, but not before several thousand believed.

"The Spirit blows where He chooses," Jesus had told them before they killed Him, "and you hear the sound of it, but you do not know where it comes from or where it goes."[3]

Did I believe in a God who behaves in such a way, who rushes in when I least expect it? Was He still sweeping through windows and starting fires? Could it be that Jesus waited for me on the detours and in the distant places with a matchbook in His hand? I did not know for sure, but I wanted to.

As my heart cried for God's tangible touch, God's words spoken through Jeremiah welled up inside of me: "Call to me, and I will answer you. I'll tell you marvelous and wondrous things that you could never figure out on your own."[4]

The voices in the foyer had long since departed, and I was now alone in the dimness of the worship center. My hands were folded in my lap, and a prayer traveled from my heart up my windpipe.

"God, show up and surprise me," I whispered.

No one answered back.

"Show up and surprise me," I said, volume rising. "I want to experience You in unexpected ways. Show up."

Job prayed a similar prayer once in a time of spiritual struggle, desperate for God's presence and voice. He'd asked God to show up amidst his sufferings and speak to him. Like most ancient Hebrews, Job knew that encountering the Holy could very well mean death. But he decided to take his chances. He'd rather die than live with the longing.

Though I didn't feel I was risking death or even devastation, my soul seemed to signal the gravity of my request. And yet not fully. For like Job, God would hear my prayer, and He would show up. And the experience would leave me...

Breathless.

Terrified.

Free.

1

Christ in the Desert

Encountering Jesus in Silence

We need to find God, and He cannot be found in noise and restlessness. God is the friend of silence.

—Mother Teresa

'd been wondering how to begin my quest to experience God in fresh ways when my phone rang. My friend Carolyn was about to take a retreat to a Benedictine monastery near her childhood hometown. The more she talked about this inconspicuous hermitage nestled in New Mexico's high desert, the more intrigued I became.

Monastery of Christ in the Desert seemed the perfect starting point for my journey because it is about as different from my suburban Atlanta home as I can imagine. I envisioned orange mesas rising out of the dirt while red-tailed hawks soared overhead. Additionally, a Benedictine monastery is a strange place for a Southern Baptist to search for God because I grew up thinking that Catholics weren't actually Christians.

I interrupted Carolyn midsentence to declare I'd be joining her on the trip. An adventurous woman by nature, she thought it was a great idea. Less than a month later, my belly full of butterflies, I boarded a plane.

I'd determined to do a silent retreat, taking a vow of quietude from the time of my arrival to departure. The monastery's Web site tempted me:

> The world is immersed in a "noise culture." People conditioned by this culture have experienced uneasiness and even fear of solitude. Here in the monastery, we hope to help you

turn off the "noise" in order to tune in to God. To quote Psalm 46:10, "Be still and know that I am God."

When modern Western Christians want to encounter God, we usually make sound. We sing or preach sermons or pray or attend a Bible study discussion to speak an "Amen." Taking the opposite approach seemed an appropriate way to begin my spiritual quest. For sixty hours, I would refrain from speaking, taking the Psalmist's advice to listen for God's voice rather than talk.

When my plane landed, the sun had risen to the height of my unease. I met up with Carolyn, and we decided to take the scenic route. For almost nine hours, we found excuses to stop by coffee shops, dine at restaurants, and detour to every tourist attraction in the self-proclaimed "Land of Enchantment." Long after sunset, we spotted a rickety sign with an arrow directing us down a dirt road.

Our car snaked through the dark canyon on the thirteen-mile "driveway" that takes almost an hour to travel. With each tire turn, our cell phone signals faded until they disappeared. By the time we pulled up to the modest guesthouse, I felt totally cut off from civilization.

A wooden gate opened into a courtyard where I picked up a Coleman lantern and made my way to the door bearing my name. The room reminded me of a jail cell, similar in size with cold concrete floors and walls. A handmade desk nested against the back wall under a three-foot square window, which let in the tiniest bit of moonlight. A string of rosary beads fell limp over a petite chair and a bearably soft twin bed lay underneath just enough blankets to keep a guest from catching cold. A wooden medallion on a leather band was draped atop my bed pillow with a note taped to it:

> Gentle Guest: If you wish to observe a stricter silence during part or all of your time here, WEAR THIS MEDALLION. The other guests and monks will respect your desire for silence. If someone does not respect your silence, please let us know. When you leave, please leave this medallion for the next guest who may also wish to have silence.
>
> Thank you! God bless!

(I learned quickly during my stay that I needed to keep the necklace with me at all times. The second day, I forgot to wear it and stopped by the kitchen to fill a water bottle. One of the older monks asked me how my stay was going. When I only smiled in response, he joked to another guest that I was "hard of hearing." I bit my lip.)

"Well, friend," I said, sizing up my new companion. "It looks like you and I are going to be spending a good bit of time together."

Having spoken my last words, I placed the medallion around my neck and unpacked my clothes.

The next morning, I woke before dawn to attend a prayer service in the oratory. Still half-asleep, Carolyn and I chose seats close to the wood-burning stove to steal a little heat while the monks, dressed in black hooded robes, filed in one by one. I fought to avoid commenting on the unusualness of the setting or how much I wished to be back in my bed, literally having to press my lips like a clamp at one point.

When I decided to travel to Christ in the Desert, I knew I was in for a bit of a shock. After all, a saying among monastery dwellers is, "If there's anything you need, let us know and we'll teach you to live without." But crossing the boundary from the noisy world to a silent space was more startling than I expected. The transition from rush to hush is not easy. Like pulling the emergency brake on a semitruck in full motion, my body screeched to a halt. With every step, my mind raced to fill the void. I'd say prayers in my head, but found I could only fill the space for a few seconds. I'd try to sit still but my knees would bounce, and I'd want to pace. *Perhaps this whole silence thing wasn't such a good idea after all.*

As the service progressed, the sun began to rise and my soul began to settle. Through the windows above, beams of light uncovered mountains hidden by darkness moments earlier. Each cliff a riot of white and red hues smearing down their rocky faces as if they'd been painted just before a rain shower. I felt like Dorothy must have when she opened the storm-beaten door and first experienced Oz in Technicolor.

My mind rejoined the service just as the monks were singing from Psalm 51: "Create in me a pure heart, O God, and put a new and loyal spirit in me." And then from Psalm 63: "O God, you are my God, and I long for you. My whole being desires you; I thirst for you, my whole being longs for you, in a dry and parched land where there is no water."

Their chants echoed the prayer I'd prayed for God to show up and speak to me. In this liturgy, I felt confirmation that God had heard my request. The tension inside me broke and the grip of worries, frustrations, and expectations loosened. My heart's ears were now opened.

. . .

Benedictines observe seven offices—or prayer times—a day.[1] As Benedict taught, "Let nothing be preferred to the work of God."[2] So prayer is made the top priority. This differs from life on the outside, where we often offer abbreviated or truncated prayers so we can rush off to work or feed our famished bellies. Not so here, where prayer is the "work" of the monastery.

This also meant my time with them marked the closest I'd ever been to what the apostle Paul called "ceaseless prayer."[3] In bed, I offered gratitude to God for the day. As I showered in the morning, I asked God's blessings on the day. When I walked the dusty paths, I pondered gifts for which to thank Him. At worship times, I praised God for being good and gracious and communicative. But best of all were the times when I just listened. This was a new way to pray for me. In His presence, my silence conveyed my trust in and dependence on Him.[4] Sometimes God spoke to my heart and at others He remained as quiet as I. This kind of prayer was not like sitting in front of a transistor radio waiting for a call, but more like wrapping oneself in a blanket fresh out of the dryer. The amazing thing about God is that He can say so much without saying anything at all.

Morning prayer is followed by breakfast, usually a slice of homemade bread smeared with peanut butter, in the refectory. All meals are eaten in silence, but the light meal (usually dinner) was accompanied by classical music and the main meal (usually lunch) featured a monk reading aloud from books like Chesterton's *Aquinas*—highbrow works that used words like "sophistry" and "fastidious" as if they were common conjunctions.

In the Benedictine tradition, you make a vow to the place, not just the order. These monks have committed to life with this community, an obligation that nonmonastic Christians like myself could learn from. I'm tempted to treat my faith community like a pair of blue jeans—something I'm keen to keep around so long as it stays in fashion or fits me or makes me look good.

This vow also teaches them to resolve issues. No other option is available. When you eat in the refectory, there is no hierarchy, and monks are not allowed to sit in cliques. Everyone sits according to how long they've been a part of the community. If the monk next to you slurps his soup, you best learn to get over it. He may be slurping in your ear for the rest of your life.

The monks' established rhythms of prayer, meals, and chores provided a new perspective on scheduling my day. Time, in modern life, seems an enemy. I struggle against him and wish to stretch him. I choke every last second out of him and then curse him for not providing more of himself. I grow frustrated as I "race against time" and "wonder where time went." Whatever time may be, he is not a friend.

But in this place, time is embraced as an honored companion. He is directed and maximized. The sun rises during morning prayer, washing the altar with incense-soaked rays. It sets during evening prayer as guests ready themselves for the evening meal. At the monastery, guests learn to settle into time's natural grooves. To move with it, rather than against it. Time is geared toward purpose, not productivity.[5]

At the end of each day, I felt as if every moment had been properly stewarded. The day wasn't a minute longer, but it seemed richer. The day was no longer governed by unexpected stimuli but rather prioritized rest and study, worship and work.

When I wasn't attending a prayer service or eating with the monks, I'd wander the grounds—reflecting, observing, listening for God's voice. The desert is visibly and audibly deafening. The sun's rays dance off the landscape and continue until dusk, when they too break for rest. The world was so still that I started wondering if I'd heard the animals whispering to each other from behind the bushes.

I started to realize that this wasn't such a strange place to encounter God after all. In Scripture, the desert is often God's chosen meeting place. He called Abraham and commissioned Moses in the desert. He led John the Baptist to dwell there, converted Paul there, and allowed Jesus to be tested there. With God, the desert often becomes a sacred space, and in each divine desert encounter, the person leaves changed.

Maybe God meets people in the desert for a reason. The vastness of its scale reminds me of my smallness. Its immortality—the desert remains as it was since before I existed and will remain until those final days—uncovers visitors' finitude. In an age where everything is torn down and rebuilt in perpetuation, the desert reminds us that some things are forever and that blessings live all around us. The mountains stretch halfway to the sky, reminding visitors that every bird, every tree, every sunset, provides reason to genuflect.

The desert is also wild and dangerous. One must look out for rattlesnakes and potholes. In the desert, a rainstorm can wash out a road without warning, and a drought can choke out life. Winds can blind, and wildlife can strike if unexpectedly threatened. Extreme temperatures are the norm—hot days reach the boiling point and nights dip into the teens or lower.

Like God, the desert moves as it wishes, and all who dare to encounter it must heed its warnings. A guest who went hiking alone now rests in the monastery's graveyard as a warning to all who treat her flippantly. Coyotes howled just outside my window at night, and if you step in the wrong ant pile, you might never step again. Such a setting forces visitors to walk on their tiptoes.

On Sundays, the monks have a full Catholic mass—something I felt uneasy about partaking in but was too curious to skip. So I joined Carolyn in our regular seats next to the woodstove. With wide eyes, I soaked up the prayers, inhaled the incense, and pondered the icons and imagery, all the while waiting to hear the abbot's sermon.

Strangely, he preached about the end times, something I would have expected from an evangelical pastor, not a Benedictine monk. He said the whole world will end one day, but in a sense, it is ending all the time. We can die at any moment, and somewhere someone is gasping for their final breath.

"God wants you awake," the abbot said, "so wake up from your stupor. He has given you another chance today to accept His gift of grace and give Him back your life."

The sermon included one of the simplest and clearest articulations of the Christian good news that I'd ever heard. His description of grace shattered my childhood notions of Catholics as work-based apostates, and left Carolyn wiping tears from her chin.

* * *

For sixty hours, I lived alert, listening for the divine voice. One afternoon, my feet crunched along the gravel path through the guesthouse courtyard, where a charred log had been set upright and carved into a statue of a monk. His branch-hands stretched heavenward and a rope tied around his middle section served as a belt. I sat in a small chair in the log-monk's shadow as the sun was setting, listening to the sounds of my breathing. And that's when my heart heard it.

"Rest in me."

I had been reading the Gospel of Matthew earlier—"Come to me, all you who are weary and burdened, and I will give you rest"—and this seemed to echo that exhortation. I needed to stop and . . .

Rest.

In.

God.

For months, I'd been rushing rather than resting. As my work-load increased, my spiritual and social lives were being squeezed and snipped. But God wanted me to pause. To take a spiritual and physical breather. In Him, no less. I had busied myself, trying to build a career and sustain a social life, and I was running on empty. But God reminded me that He wanted to take all that weariness and burden from me and replace it with a more trusting disposition.

I won't write of every shared moment with God while at the monastery. Doing so would somehow violate the intimacy we enjoyed. Besides, describing with words what happens when one meets God in silence is something of an impossible feat. It can only be experienced. But these first words God spoke to my heart are hard to keep to myself.

Perhaps God had been speaking these words for weeks or months, but only now was I able to receive them. Could I have heard these words anywhere? Maybe. God *can* shout over noise. But being in a silent state helped me to hear, unclogging my ears. Without the raucous world around me, I could discern God's voice. As the monks often remind their guests, "One cannot listen to the Divine while one is talking."

Inhabitants of the modern world often fear silence and solitude. Having bathed in chaos, quiet spaces become a kind of wilderness or uncharted frontier. We run from soundlessness because it makes us most uncomfortable.

Recently, I tried yoga for the first time. I found the most difficult pose not to be downward-facing dog or warrior, but the first. The pose where participants must be still and listen to the sound of their own breathing. I preferred the pain of twisted and stretched sinews to the peace of stillness. But I'm like most people, I guess, whose first inclination when they see silence approaching is to turn and run.

As my desert retreat taught me, in those moments I must resist the desire to flee and instead pursue God there, expecting that when I listen He will speak.

Interestingly, when the noise of life drives me to the brink of insanity, I often self-medicate with more of the nasty virus. I turn on music or a film. I call a friend and yap for a while. When this doesn't help, I assume this must be my lot in life. If only I could embrace more hushful moments, I might discover that freedom is just two closed lips away.

For the Christian, silence is more than an effort to retreat from noise. It is an opportunity to lean into God. To sense His presence in life, to notice the contours of His intervention, to express our reliance on Him.

"It's good to spend time in silence," one monk told me. "So long as you've got one ear tuned to the Lord."

Self-induced quietude is not a doorway to descend into oneself. Rather than brooding introspection, it creates worship turned outward and upward. Solitude is not an attempt to run away from life's noise and distractions as much as an attempt to run to the God who often waits beyond such things. Before I came to the desert, I believed a monastery to be a place one went to empty themselves of pleasure and desire, but I could not have been more wrong. This was a filling station, not a siphon.

That is why the monks guard it so fiercely. They have a strict ban on instruments and radios and cell phones. They want silence to be as commonplace inside the monastery as chaos is outside of it. Even the pace of the prayers often takes visitors off guard, so the monastery offers the following advice:

"When we leave the monastery, it is the outside world that seems to be rushing along too quickly. Slow down, brothers and sisters. God is not going anywhere."

• • •

In the Gospel of Luke, we stumble across a crusty old priest named Zechariah. I imagine him hunched over with knuckles hardened by rheumatoid arthritis, faithfully executing his duties in the temple despite the pains of old age. Zechariah's feet shuffle from the sacrificed flesh to the altar day after day. At home, his wife, Elizabeth, fights off depression. She is barren, shamed in the eyes of the community due to never having given birth.

One day, Zechariah's division is on duty and, according to Jewish custom, his lot is chosen to enter the temple and burn incense. Crowds of worshipers are praying outside, but his failing ears can barely hear their muffled voices. When his hand stretches to set fire to the incense, he notices another figure standing next to the altar. Something is different about this man—so different that Zechariah knows he has not merely wandered in. This is an angel of the Lord, a fact that forces the priest to fall to the floor.

"Do not be afraid, Zechariah, for your prayer has been heard, and your wife, Elizabeth, will bear you a son, and you shall call his name 'John,'" the angel declares. "And you will have joy and gladness, and many will rejoice at His birth, for He will be great before the Lord."[6]

Luke says Zechariah is a righteous man, but the spirit of Father Abraham wells up inside of him. *Doesn't he know how old we are? My wife and I are pruney, dried-up, no longer able to conceive a child. Maybe a younger man was supposed to draw the lot today.*

Then the angel responds to Zechariah's disbelief in the most peculiar way:

"I am Gabriel. I stand in the presence of God, and I have been sent to speak to you and to tell you the good news. And now you will be silent and not able to speak until the day this happens, because you did not believe my words, which will come true at their appointed time."

Having first encountered this passage as a child, I assumed God was punishing Zechariah through Gabriel for probing the prophecy further. After all, I thought, God dislikes being questioned. But after encountering the Bible more broadly, I think more might be happening here. After all, Scripture records many questioners who are not disciplined. Mary even questions the same angel at her annunciation and is not struck silent.

I now wonder if striking Zechariah mute was both a punishment and a gift. Rather than simmering over being questioned, maybe God knew Zechariah better than we. The priest's flapping jaws were busy speaking, inquiring, and arguing, and God knew that he needed to stop talking in order to fully hear what

God was saying, in order to receive what God was about to do in his midst.

Jesus also knew the importance of intentional quiet when discerning God's voice, and we have record of Him seeking it out more than half a dozen times. Sometimes Jesus would climb a mountain, at others He would take a wilderness retreat or a boat ride. But often Jesus would withdraw to what the Gospelers called "a lonely place."[7]

Jesus wasn't alone in seeing the value of such things. Isaiah prophesied, "In repentance and rest you shall be saved, in quietness and trust."[8] Zechariah demanded, "Be silent, all people, before the Lord."[9] Habakkuk stood silently beside the city guard post listening and looking for God. Once Elijah put the kibosh on his whining, he heard God come in a "still, small voice." After Paul was converted, he didn't begin preaching. He went to Arabia for a quiet retreat of his own.

With such a rich tradition, no wonder ancient Christians practiced silence and solitude more often than we. A group of Christians called the Desert Fathers and Mothers fled to the wildernesses of Syria, Egypt, and Palestine in the third century. Here they lived in caves, on mountaintops, and in abandoned tombs.[10] They took drastic measures to rely on God, trust in God, and listen for God's voice—all the while promoting neighbor-love as an alternative lifestyle. They kept the Bible close to their hearts, interpreting it, not just through scholarship, but also by attempting to live it out.[11]

By living in lonely places, the Desert Fathers and Mothers embodied a practice many Christians have long since forgotten. But during my visit to the desert, I couldn't help feeling that I'd connected with them in some way. And with Zechariah, for, like the old priest, I'd discovered that what first seems like difficulty is often a present in disguise.

. . .

The dawning sun was just beginning to peek through my bedroom window as I packed my bags to depart. When I arrived several days earlier, my muscles were tense from stress and I carried a suitcase full of anxiety. Now I felt relaxed and refilled. From the abbot's sermon at mass to God's urging to rest in Him, I felt like I'd had a genuine encounter with God in a way I'd never imagined possible. I went looking for an "aha" moment with flashes of light and a baritone voice from heaven. But instead, I experienced an "ahhh" moment.

Yet, what I experienced at the monastery can be had in other places as well. The same posture can be nurtured in cities and suburbs as in the desert. Christian mystic Henri Nouwen said that while we may withdraw to physical solitude for periods of time, what really matters is "solitude of the heart."[12] And I felt like I had achieved this. Or at least grazed it. But I didn't feel like I had to abandon it just because I was departing.

Pilgrims mustn't trek to a wilderness cloister. They can turn off the TV and stop creating background noise. They can replace an hour of video games or Internet surfing with a moment or two engaging Scripture. They can take time to pause and ponder the good works of God that are too easily overlooked. And they can learn to grow comfortable with God in lonely places, much like our Lord did.

After my experience, I'm convinced I need to embrace regular times of silence in life. Not passive silence, where the back is turned and the arms are folded, but active silence, where my ears are open and palms are turned toward the sky. Maybe God waits to meet me in that space, though I had never conceived of such a thing.

After my bags were packed, I grabbed the wooden medallion dangling from my neck. He and I had been nearly inseparable during my stay, and I considered taking him with me. We'd spent so much time together, and I didn't want to say farewell. But in the end, I knew the next pilgrim needed him more than I. So I slid him over my head and placed him atop the pillow where we'd first met.

My only regret was that I never got to say good-bye to everyone. I wished I could have spoken with Brother Andre, the guest-master who'd made me feel so welcome. Or the abbot, whose honest sermon had split me in two. Or the baker, whose crusty loaves gave me strength to face each day. Before departing, I wish I could have told them thanks.

But maybe I didn't need to. They'd seen me arrive and depart hundreds of times. Wanderers of various names who'd come to the desert with butterflies in their bellies and left with full hearts.

2

And a Mighty Wind Blows

Encountering Jesus in His Sanctuary

People encounter God under shady oak trees, on river-banks, at the tops of mountains, and in long stretches of barren wilderness. God shows up in whirlwinds, starry skies, burning bushes, and perfect strangers.

—BARBARA BROWN TAYLOR

When I purchased my home, I had few requirements, but one was that the backyard butt up against trees. Too many homes in suburban Atlanta, where I live, are built on tiny parcels of land with a few trees sprinkled artificially along the road, but almost no original woodlands. I wanted something more, and when I found it, I bought it.

My back porch has since become a sanctuary—a place I pray and pause, read the Scriptures, and sing praises to God. Many mornings I step outside, coffee in hand, and belt an old hymn remembered from my childhood. My neighbors who work from home must think me crazy.

One memorable morning, I sang a hymn that draws its lyrics from Psalm 8:

> *O Lord, Our Lord.*
> *How majestic is your name in all the earth!*
> *O Lord, we praise your name.*
> *O Lord, we magnify your name,*
> *Prince of Peace, Mighty God.*
> *O Lord God Almighty.*

I've warbled this refrain in the early hours of the morning dozens of times, but something was different this day. As I sang, the sound of rushing traffic heard from the street faded. Daybreak gave way to stillness, and I felt as if I was no longer alone. As the melody flowed, a mighty wind blew, sweeping up leaves and grass clippings. The Georgia pines stretching above my head began to sway back and forth as if to worship with me.

I grew up thinking only mystics and pagans encountered God in nature, and yet here I was and here God seemed to be. My curiosity outgrew my confusion, and I continued to sing while the trees danced along. When the chorus concluded and the last note was sung, I stopped. And so did the wind. The whooshing sound of speeding cars returned, and I knew I was alone again.

Could this be? Had God met me in a suburban Atlanta neighborhood?

For several days, I processed what happened, never sharing the experience with others. When I could no longer keep it to myself, I recounted the event to a friend, assuming she'd think me bonkers. Instead, she recited a passage of Scripture:

"Praise God in His sanctuary; praise God in His mighty heavens...Let everything that has breath praise the Lord."[1]

Like me, those trees have breath. They inhale and purify the air before exhaling it. Like me, they had been created for God's glory. Perhaps the Creator met me that morning in His sanctuary.

But why?

John Muir had a similar experience once, and he reflected afterward: "A few minutes ago every tree was excited, bowing to the roaring storm, waving, swirling, tossing their branches in glorious enthusiasm like worship. But though to the outer ear these trees are now silent, their songs never cease."

Maybe God wanted to remind me that He is everywhere despite my best efforts to contain Him. He often waits in the common places, but with God the familiar can become unfamiliar with a single gust of wind. He is like the Lion in Lewis's Narnia, going and coming when and where He pleases. I needed to live alert. If God could appear in my suburban backyard, perhaps He could arise anywhere.

· · ·

Through the lens of Scripture, my God encounter didn't seem so strange. God often revealed Himself to people in nature. He met Elisha and John the Baptist in the wilderness. He spoke to Moses through a shrub and Noah in a freshly cut twig. If Job wanted to probe the depth of his Creator, God said, "Ask the animals, and they will teach you, or the birds of the air, and they will tell you; or speak to the earth, and it will teach you, or let the fish of the sea inform you."[2]

Jesus even said if you want a novel encounter with God, pay attention to the birds of the air and lilies of the field. When He wanted to spend time with the Father, Jesus was known to climb mountains or hike into the rough country to watch the sun rise. This was a man born in a manger and warmed by farm animals. When He wanted to drive a lesson home, He'd pluck wheat or describe the planting of crops.

Some modern Christians have disremembered the God who considers the whole world His sanctuary. But this God was the One worshipped for centuries by Christians like Augustine and Bonaventure and St. Francis. We've forgotten the words of the venerated Church father Tertullian, who said, "Nature is schoolmistress, the soul the pupil." Or the great reformer

Martin Luther, who commented, "God writes the Gospel not in the Bible alone, but also on trees, and in the flowers and clouds and stars."

We overlook a God who makes poppies and poplars grow. We forget that we worship One who can show up in the scent of cedar bark, the sweetness of wild blackberries, or the sound of wind rustling leaves sacrificed to autumn. This God is unlike the One so many of us have created, discontent with hiding out in church buildings until we find the time to pay Him a visit.

Perhaps one of the most spectacular God-stories ever told involves a stubborn little man named Jonah. It reads like a tragi-comedy because Jonah was a colossal jerk. He was the first and worst foreign missionary, and if Norman Vincent Peale had written Jonah's biography it would have been titled *The Power of Negative Thinking*.[3] Yet God finds a way to make use of the unlikely prophet, a fact that encourages all imperfect God servants thousands of years later.

Jonah may have had friends—we don't know—but he doesn't seem to like people very much. When God asks him to tell the Ninevites that God plans on wiping them out, he balks. Nineveh was the capital of Assyria, and as such, was the geographical personification of wickedness for the Hebrew people. To avoid God's instructions, Jonah goes AWOL and boards a ship sailing for Tarshish. By heading in the opposite direction, Jonah thinks he will flee the presence of the Almighty.

But a funny thing happened on the way to Tarshish. A storm arises, threatening to capsize the vessel. With thunder clapping, Jonah confesses to the crew that he is the cause of the storm, and the seamen waste no time tossing him overboard. That's when events grow interesting, because a great fish opens his great mouth and swallows the not-so-great prophet.

For three days, Jonah languishes in the stench of the whale's belly, and here God teaches him a lesson we'd all do well to learn: you cannot escape God. Where can we go where God is not? He pursues us wherever we go, whether on a ship sailing for Tarshish or on a suburban back porch.

The Psalmist later lyricized the idea:

> *Where can I go from your Spirit?*
> *Where can I flee from your presence?*
> *If I go up to the heavens, You are there; if I make my bed*
>   *in the depths, You are there.*
> *If I rise on the wings of the dawn, if I settle on the far*
>   *side of the sea,*
> *Even there Your hand will guide me, Your right hand*
>   *will hold me fast.*
> *If I say, "Surely the darkness will hide me and the light*
>   *become night around me,"*
> *Even the darkness will not be dark to You; the night will*
>   *shine like the day, for darkness is as light to You.*[4]

Sitting on stomach lining and surrounded by fish bones, Jonah finally repents, and the whale vomits the prophet up. Jonah wastes no time traveling to Nineveh, but though his location has changed, his attitude hasn't. Pastor Stephen Shoemaker suggests that if a movie were made of Jonah, Danny DeVito would be perfect cast as the prophet, traipsing through town announcing judgment, barely able to hide his glee at their impending destruction.[5]

Jonah preaches, and his worst fears come true. The pagans repent, and God offers them the same rope of mercy He gave Jonah. The book of Jonah ends with the prophet sulking, as he is wont to do, and readers are left to chew on the book's great lessons.

First, God has a penchant for imperfect servants. Jonah is not an exception; he is the rule. The Bible is a series of narratives where God uses short-tempered, shortsighted, and utterly flawed people to accomplish His will. There was Moses the fugitive, Rahab the prostitute, Samson the player, Jacob the deceiver, Naomi the depressed, Thomas the doubter, Paul the murderer, and Peter the impulsive. Each is an unlikely disciple, but God has a habit of restoring the world through broken people.

Jonah's story reminds me that God's grace is available to even the most stubborn among us. When I run from it, grace chases after me. When I turn my back to it, grace taps me on the shoulder. When I fold my arms to it, grace tackles me with a warm bear hug.

Finally, the story of Jonah exposes my desire to place limitations on God. Jonah believed God could be geographically constrained, and I often make similar mistakes. I might constrain God chronologically: "He may have worked that way in the Bible, but He can't work that way now." Or theologically: "God can't do that because it violates the system I've accepted." Or intellectually: "That can't be true of God because it doesn't make sense to me."

But God constraints lead to more than conceptual problems. They limit how far and deep I can go in my relationship with

God. They shift my focus to the boundaries I've built instead of probing the edges of spiritual possibility. Before I know it, I'm compressed and pretzelized, exhausted by the confinements I've placed on God and myself.

But as the grumpy prophet reminds me, my limitless God loves breaking out of the prisons I construct for Him. If I find myself in a fish's belly buried under miles of ocean, God still sits beside me. Even if I rise on the wings of the dawn or settle on the far side of the sea, God waits for me there. *Keep your eyes peeled,* Jonah might say to me, *for God will show up when you least expect Him.*

. . .

About a month after my surprise encounter in nature, I tried to re-create the experience. I rose when the sun was just waking, brewed a cup of coffee, and stepped outside. Taking a deep breath, I exhaled the same song. With each word, I waited for God to show up, but He never came. The trees continued to snore—perhaps it was too early for pines to dance—and the wind did not blow. A squirrel looked at me with confusion, and a woodpecker chipped into a broken limb above.

Confused, I snatched up my coffee cup and sulked inside. *Why wasn't I able to re-create the experience as before? Did I misread the experience? Maybe the occurrence was all in my head?*

But then I realized that my second effort was little more than an attempt to force God's hand. I was trying to manipulate God: "You worked like this before. You *must* work like this again." How often do I relate to God in such a way, as a magician I can call on when I want a magic trick? Though I assumed I was releasing God that day, my actions were ironically an attempt to contain Him. God shows up in His timing and not mine, how He wants, but rarely at my beckoning. Even the Pevensie kids couldn't push through the wardrobe every time they tried.

"Left to ourselves," A. W. Tozer once wrote, "we tend to reduce God to manageable terms. We want to get Him where we can use Him, or at least know where He is when we need Him. We want a God we can, in some measure, control."[6]

More than half a century after Tozer penned those words, Christians like me have proved him right. We keep striving to develop detailed and systematized explanations of God, to distill the Creator of the universe down to a handful of pithy one-liners and acronyms. We even read books about God that are many times longer than the ones He wrote about himself.

God wanted to wow me and woo me and love me and surprise me, but I wanted to manage Him. He wanted to expand my capacity to encounter Him, and I wanted to control Him. No wonder the relationship often grows strained.

With my windy worship experience and failed second attempt fresh in my heart, I stooped to pray:

Father, expose the areas where I've been asking for a magic trick. Reveal the ways I've tried to bottle or shrink-wrap you. Break out of the boxes I've built around you. Send your wind to sweep me off my feet and take my breath away.

Amen.

3

Cereal Snowflakes

Encountering Jesus in Mystery

*It would seem very strange that Christianity should
have come into the world just to receive an explanation.*
—Søren Kierkegaard

n the midst of a bustling parking lot, I saw a familiar but forlorn face. Denise's hair was shorter this encounter than our last, and I liked her new look. She was a gregarious woman by nature—always full of jokes and wit—but today, distress wallpapered her countenance. I decided to ask what gnawed at her.

"My life is falling apart," she said.

I could taste her anguish.

Both she and her husband, Leonard, had been battling cancer, and just as they received a clean bill of health, the company he'd started years earlier could no longer pay the bills. Leonard made a deal with an investor to purchase the company with a single caveat: if they were not profitable within one year, the new owner could fire Leonard and his sons, who were in his employ. The home where they'd raised their children was put up as collateral.

The seasons passed with a blur, and the company swam in red. Leonard was handed a pink slip, and he lost his home. The couple, now well into their sixties, were forced to move into a spare bedroom in their son's house.

"That isn't the whole of it," Denise said, her eyes filling with tears.

Bella, her miniature Yorkshire terrier—more a best friend than a pet—had grown seriously ill. The thought of losing one of her life's last joys tore holes in her heart.

"I begged God to spare Bella," she said. "I told Him, 'You took my health and my home and my business, but You can't have my puppy. She's all I have left.'"

That night, Bella died and something inside Denise felt like it did too. In a near-Biblical protest, she rose from bed, slipped into the bathroom, grasped a pair of seamstress shears, and cut all her hair off.

"Jonathan, tell me why God would let this happen," she demanded. "We've served Him faithfully our whole lives, and now He's let us lose everything."

I knew better than to stitch together an answer, so we stood in silence as I watched her tears splatter on the pavement.

"My whole life, whenever I've had a question about my circumstances, I've always been able to get an answer from my pastor or my church. But no one can seem to help this time," she said.

More than anything, I wanted to give her an explanation, some shred of advice to console her. I had nothing to offer except a friend's embrace.

. . .

When I survey the wreckage of life around me, I can't help but ask similar questions as Denise. What is one to make of life when the wheels fall off the applecart? When the cancer comes or the nurse hands parents a baby with an incurable disease? When one strains to find reasonable explanations for a life lost too early? Can I believe, can I have faith, when I search for justification and come back empty-handed? Is God to be found in those moments when the answers to one's deepest inquiries cannot be found?

Modern believers are not the only ones to wrestle such questions. The Biblical authors attempted to trace God's fingerprints in the seemingly inexplicable, and they described God, His ways, and His nature as:

- Unsearchable
- Inscrutable
- Undiscoverable
- Untraceable
- Unfathomable
- Beyond measure
- Inexhaustible
- Infinite
- Beyond comprehension
- Far beyond our reach
- More than we imagine
- Past finding out
- Exalted beyond our knowledge
- One who dwells in a dark cloud and unapproachable light[1]

"Who has understood the mind of the LORD, or instructed him as counselor?" Isaiah asks.[2] The question is rhetorical, for all within earshot would have shouted back, "No one." The God I was chasing after is cloaked in mystery and no measure of squinting will resolve the image of Him seen in the distance.

I often struggle to sit in life's messiest moments, to trust God for what He's given me or allowed to flood my life. My sophomore year of high school, I struggled with the truthfulness of Christianity. Several friends had shattered the simplicity of my faith with a few well-constructed arguments, leaving me reeling spiritually.

My student pastor told me that I needed to read some apologetics books so I could argue better. I took his advice, rooting my faith in rationalism and relying on logic to help me solve faith's greatest questions. I began to explore all the "evidence that demands a verdict" and construct a "case for faith." While these efforts reminded me that my faith wasn't as silly as my skeptical friends seemed to believe, they failed to sustain me. I had boiled down the great depths of God and faith to arguments short enough to fit on an index card, easily memorized and ready to deploy in debates, and reduced my relationship with Jesus to a few bullet points to be shelved in my head and not worked out with my hands. My spirit thirsted for a supernatural encounter with a God who transcends logic.

"There are many people who reach their conclusions about life like schoolboys," Søren Kierkegaard wrote in his journal. "They cheat their master by copying the answer out of a book without having worked out the sum for themselves."[3]

Faith in God isn't *irrational*, but it is sometimes *suprarational*.[4] That is, faith often transcends logic. While apologetics can be good and helpful, my experience has been that they are insufficient. Spiritual arguments are a runway too short to launch the plane of faith. At the end of the logical pavement is a stretch of asphalt called "mystery," and it can only be traveled, not explained.

In recent years, I've quit reducing and started living my faith instead. In those places where I brush up against the Holy, I find an apologetic that is difficult to explain but as real as my reflection in a mirror. The longer I chase after God in this way, the more convinced I am that God is more than accessible or complex. He is mysterious, which is to say He can be known but not comprehended, experienced but never fully explained. We look but don't see clearly, reach but never grasp.

Though the Bible can seem like a relatively large book, it is less than a pamphlet of what might be said about God. If there were a full record of God's workings and description of His nature, it would comprise more books than could be contained in every e-reader on earth. And even if I could access such a collection of facts and stories about God and memorize each one, I could not fully grasp it.

Imagine that you had taught an elementary-aged child about biology by helping her grow a bean sprout under a heat lamp. If you then placed that child in a graduate botany course, she would fail every test. Why? Because the amount and complexity of information would be too great for the child's mind to comprehend.

The metaphor Christians have used for centuries to explain the way humans encounter such a God is seeing. Though every object can be seen, humans cannot see every object. Some objects cannot be clearly viewed with human eyes. The best example might be the earth's sun, which is on the one hand visible and on the other never glimpsed for a prolonged period of time. Though the sun is visible, it dazzles the eyes. It overcomes, forcing one to look away. What the sun is to human eyes, God is to our human minds.[5]

But if I cannot fully take in God and His ways, should I throw up my hands and avoid Him altogether? Is encountering God a waste of my time, an exercise in impossibility? The answer seems to be no.

In order to experience such a thing to the fullest of my capacities, I attempt to comprehend whatever I can while recognizing that a God worth worshipping can never be boiled down to neat rationalizations. Instead, He must be experienced and embraced. When I attempt to understand God through human reason, I am approaching Him, not explaining Him. At some point, I should expect to run out of highway. In these moments, I must stop analyzing and begin receiving. Rather than reducing God to a series of rigid dogmatics, I must learn to sit in His warm rays and soak up the heat He radiates.

Scripture says that the mystery of God has been revealed, but in being made known He has not ceased to be a mystery. This holy unknowable is not a puzzle to be solved but rather meant to be embraced *as* a mystery. When Jesus refers to the apostles as those who have "been given the mystery of the kingdom of God," He is not saying that they've been given some grand, but unsolvable puzzle, or a question to which there is no answer. He is saying that the mystery *is* the solution. It *is* the answer.[6] Even as I embrace God and He reveals Himself to me, the mystery remains mysterious.

Rather than grow frustrated, I should celebrate this truth about God because it means there's always more of Him to uncover and discover. His mysterious nature is a great gift, beckoning me to go deeper in my relationship with Him, forcing me to live on high alert, and making me recognize that even when I think I know Him, there's always more.

Embracing mystery means acknowledging how much I don't know, admitting how small a piece of the puzzle I hold, and yet accepting that through it all God can still be trusted.

Sometimes, it seems, the question *is* the answer.

. . .

When I met Denise and Leonard for dinner a few months after our first encounter in the parking lot, Denise had a new countenance. The heaviness was still there, but the shadow over her face wasn't so dark. She told me that she had stopped waiting for a full explanation to her problems and instead was trusting God in the absence of answers. In her new posture, she was experiencing God in unexpected ways.

God was growing and stretching her faith, teaching her to derive joy from relationships rather than circumstances. Her family, which had been strained in years past, was drawn closer together than ever before as they grieved the losses they'd experienced. Rather than focus on life's problems, they were learning to look for God's provision in the midst of it all.

As the waitress laid down a bit of hummus and a basket of pita, the Biblical image of bread came to my mind. In the book of Exodus, the Israelites are liberated from their Egyptian captivity only to enter another captivity of sorts. They become prisoners of the desert, aimless wanderers in a dreary landscape of sand and blistering sun, plunged into their own season of searching.

Halfway through the second month, everyone grows restless. *Where is this "promised land" Moses told us about? Does it even exist?*

Food is sparse, and though their bellies growl, their complaints roar even louder:

"At least when we were slaves in Egypt, we had food to eat."

God hears their cries and tells Moses that He will make bread rain down from heaven. The Israelites must go out and gather only enough to survive that day, except the sixth day of the week, when they would collect a double portion to last through the Sabbath. This divine bread became symbolic of God's provision for His people. They even kept a two-quart jar of it inside the ark of the covenant next to the Ten Commandments, so they would never forget that God provided for them like stray kittens that wandered to the divine doorstep each morning looking for a saucer of milk.

In the repetition of the gift, I learn that God often comes in the mundane and the rote. God is made known in the average and the everyday. The sunrise that meets me in the morning and the friendly wave of the mailwoman. The greeting from the receptionist as I shuffle to a meeting and the hug from the retiree who waits for me at the church door each Sunday after service. Jesus shows up in the mystery of crisis and the rhythm of the ordinary.

Perhaps each morning when I throw back my covers, I should begin searching for manna, for those seemingly routine blessings that God has placed on my doorstep. Maybe I should become a scavenger for God's kept promises that I might otherwise brush past or skip over. I gather only what I need, accepting that God is in it even when I don't understand.

But there is more to this narrative than a story of God's provision. The bread was called "manna," a name derived from the Hebrew "man hu," which literally translates to "What is it?" Even though the Israelites didn't know what it was or how it got there, each morning they gathered and ate the mysterious bread because they trusted God. In so doing, they illustrated how those who follow God must live each day, embracing life's circumstances—even those not understood—believing they have passed through heaven.

Faith calls me to welcome the mysterious, to rest in the uncomfortable tension of a God who is both known and unknown. This kind of faith doesn't require an explanation for why I'm wandering in the wilderness; rather, it trusts in the God of the wilderness despite the absence of answers.

Some mornings, the meal at my feet may not look very appetizing. Sometimes it may even turn my stomach. I suppose I know how the Israelites felt in those moments. The downside of their miracle meal was its sameness. Manna for Monday lunch and Wednesday dinner. Manna for breakfast on Saturday. And all day Sunday. Three meals per day for forty years, they ate what one theologian called "cereal snowflakes."[7] That is, 43,800 manna meals with no break. The author of Exodus says manna was "like coriander seed, white, and the taste of it was like wafers made with honey."[8] The description sounds pretty appetizing at first, but even honey wafers get old when you eat them every meal.

Interestingly, God never gets angry at the Israelites for wanting this food or even for asking. He created them with a desire for nourishment and then led them into the desert, where food was sparse. They asked, and God gave. The rub came when they hoarded food even though He promised to provide a fresh supply each morning. Their natural desire for nourishment grew into an entitlement to receive it on their own terms and a disbelief that God would provide as promised. Similarly, my natural desire for life to make sense is not wrong. Where it can cripple me is when I refuse to trust God to provide the answers I *really* need, *when* I truly need them.

The lesson in these manna meals continues into the New Testament. Paul doesn't describe Christians as people who have all the answers to every question or even those who can construct the best arguments. Instead, they are those who live by a story that doesn't always make sense and serve a God who isn't a slave to human logic. Christians are, in Paul's words, "stewards of the mysteries of God"[9] who lean on a narrative that makes us sound foolish.[10]

Humans have resisted such an interaction with God since humanity's dawning moments. In Genesis, Adam and Eve faced it. God offered for them to eat from the tree of life. This was the fruit of trust and faith and surrender. But God told them not to take from the tree of knowledge. "Eat this fruit," the serpent tempted, "and then you'll know the answers." They follow the snake's prodding, but the meal fails to satisfy.

Later on, after Moses has trusted God through the highest highs and lowest lows, he makes a most unusual request: "Show me Your glory." God responds by walking past him, but even as Moses desires to see more of God, the Almighty reveals only His back. This reaching out but never grasping is an image echoed in the woman who stretches to touch the hem of Jesus's garment and, if you're like me, is a strangely accurate picture of what following God feels like. I beg to see Him in His fullness, to look God squarely in the face. And, yes, I glimpse Him. But only His back. And somehow that is enough.

In these moments, I am reminded that I am limited in what I can know about God, but also that I can at least brush the edges and experience Him in a powerful and tangible way.[11] For when I arise with the sun to discover life's *What is it?* scattered on the ground, I can still trust that God has placed it there and that I will experience Him as I eat.

* * *

The picture of bread reemerges in the New Testament Gospels. When the peckish crowds approached Jesus, He produced more than enough of it. God gave them manna in the desert, Jesus told them, but the Father wants them to eat "true bread" from heaven.

"Give us this bread always," they begged Him.

"I am the bread of life," Jesus responded. "Whoever comes to me will never be hungry again."

Jesus fed their appetites, yes, but then He gave them what they really needed: a slice of Himself. He wanted to make sure everyone knew that "humans cannot live by bread alone." Jesus is the true manna in the wilderness. He is the holy mystery, the divine *What is it?* When hunger pangs loom large, what I really need are not answers. I need more of Him. To feast on the true bread. Jesus is better than I imagined because He transforms my desires into opportunities to experience what truly satisfies.

On the night before Jesus was arrested, the disciples gathered for a final meal, and the menu couldn't have been more perfect. Lifting a loaf of bread, Jesus gave thanks for God's provision. Then He broke it and passed it around the table.

"Take and eat," He said.

Not "Take and understand."

Through the first communion, Jesus was offering again the mystery of Himself. It must have been difficult for the disciples to understand what it all meant. He called this bread His body and the wine His blood, but they could see His body and He didn't appear to be bleeding. Jesus wanted them to push deeper than the physical images and understand the meaning behind them.

The life of faith is one where I experience all kinds of inexplicable and unexplainable situations. I ask for answers, and sometimes I receive them. Other times, I'm left to wonder. But even in these mysterious moments, Jesus is there. Broken. Blessed. Distributed. Waiting in the bread I've been handed but may not have chosen.

Will I eat?

When I'm in the wilderness of life wandering in search of my personal promised land, I face a choice. Either I will run from God because of His elusiveness or I will praise Him *because* of it. Will I reject the paradoxes and seeming absurdity of life or will I choose to exercise faith, clinging to God in the absence of answers? When I operate in certainty, I hold tightly to myself and my ability to reason well, but when I embrace mystery, I'm forced to tie myself to the ship mast of God's presence and hold fast even as life's storms rage.

Often my greatest need is not to find an answer, but to simply be. To take and eat, knowing that the miracle isn't in the gift but in the One who gives it.

Walking the halls of a church in another town recently, a man ran into me and knocked me off balance. I whipped around to see an elderly gentleman wearing dark sunglasses being led around by the arm of a woman. I knew he must be blind.

Jim was a gifted athlete growing up, and in the late 1960s, he was about to be recruited to play professional baseball. Unfortunately, like many young men during that era, his country asked him to place his dreams aside. The army drafted him to fight in the Vietnam War.

Jim agreed.

Jim was trained.

Jim deployed to the battlefield.

In the midst of a heated firefight, a bomb exploded a few feet from him, inflicting terrible wounds. When he awoke in a foreign hospital, he was informed that the blast had stolen his eyesight and most of his hearing. But hope still found its way into Jim's troubled life.

As a compassionate nurse cared for his wounds, they became fast friends and eventually fell in love. After the war, they married. She stuck by her marriage vows—caring for him, loving him, and reading him stacks of textbooks to help him earn two PhDs.

Nearly four decades later, she leads her soldier around by the hand, and Jim can't talk about his darling nurse without being gripped by emotion.

"I love my wife," Jim says, "even though I've never seen her."

That day, I was knocked back by the living embodiment of 1 Peter 1:8:

"Though you have not seen Him, you love Him; and even though you do not see Him now, you believe in Him and are filled with an inexpressible and glorious joy."

My journey with Jesus is often filled with doubt, anxiety, and dispassion. I ask for bread and He gives it, never explaining where it came from or how He plans to use it to nourish me. I strain to grasp our Savior, but touch only the hem of His robe. I squint to see Him, but catch only a glimpse of His back. I call out to Him and only hear the faintest echoes of His voice. Or perhaps nothing at all.

And yet I choose to love Him still.

To believe though blind.

I didn't know Jim's story when he bumped into me that day, but I saw a glimmer of heaven in the loving touch of his wife and the strange satisfied smile that stuck to his face. Similarly, that first morning when I saw Denise, I didn't know of her tragedy or that she had chopped off her hair in an act of protest. All I knew was that she was lovely. And isn't that just like our God? He is One who can take mysterious tragedies and transform them into something beautiful.

4

Mountains beyond Mountains

Encountering Jesus in the Impossible

Only he who can see the invisible can do the impossible.
—FRANK GAINES

The night after the catastrophic earthquake rocked Haiti's capital city of Port-au-Prince on January 10, 2010, thousands of Haitians slept outside. Over a quarter million residences were obliterated, but the estimated 220,000 deaths were the source of the wails that could be heard far into the surrounding mountains. In the Place Saint-Pierre, hundreds lay helpless under the stars singing a simple hymn: "God, you are the One who gave me life. Why are we suffering?"[1]

Their desperation would continue for months as countries around the world sent aid to the troubled island nation. And when I arrived, just before Christmas 2012, the situation still seemed dire.

Massive tent cities were assembled with USAID tarps and sheet metal. Inside one, a woman wearing men's boxer briefs as shorts used a plastic pail filled with brownish water to bathe her naked son, who was well past puberty. A sewage canal snaked past the road to compensate for the lack of trash collecting services. Horses and cows grazed on garbage heaps, a man with a leg chopped off at the knee joined a crowd of beggars asking for money or food, and we occasionally drove by automobile graveyards filled with deceased buses and Land Cruisers. The cars inhabiting it seemed as lifeless as the humans living just feet from their final resting places.

In addition to the desolation, Haiti can also be dangerous. While there, I had a terrifying experience.

I was traveling with Peter Greer, who heads HOPE International, a Christian microenterprise group that works in developing nations to provide a hand up rather than a handout. HOPE invests in the dreams of the poor by discipling them in Christ, providing financial training, and offering them microloans to start businesses or invest in their future. They believe the best way to end poverty is to fulfill our mandate to care for the "least of these" by ending charity and transitioning to a model centering on job creation and economic development.[2]

The day before I left, I woke in a small rural town named Miragoane to a breakfast of hot dog buns and peanut butter. I was still hungry from having eaten only a cup of porridge for dinner, so I was grateful to have food that morning. Some Haitians were doubtlessly going without. We had a two-and-a-half-hour trek back to Port-au-Prince, and a local who was associated with HOPE offered to drive us. Everything seemed to be going according to plan until we ran into some unexpected traffic.

The town we were passing through was protesting having been without electricity for the last three days. Two buses were blocking the highway. No one except locals was allowed through. Peter had to catch a flight that afternoon that he could not miss, so waiting wasn't an option. Our driver found a local walking by who claimed he could get us through the roadblock for one thousand *goudes*, which is roughly twenty-five U.S. dollars. That seemed fair enough, and we had no other option, so we let him climb into the driver's seat and take over.

To our relief, we were allowed to move through the buses in a matter of minutes. But we were not in the clear. The protestors had parked a semitruck across the highway and slashed the tires to immobilize it. Unfortunately, there was a ditch on one side of the road and a ravine on the other. The truck in front of us tried to squeeze around the shoulder, but it fell into the ravine. We concluded that following the same path was probably not the best idea.

The only other option was to take a "back road." It's important to note that this Haitian back road was a dirt trail carved through the jungle. After deliberation with our driver, we were assured that he could get us around the blockade using one of these trails. We agreed.

We turned left into an opening in the trees, but after bumping along a few hundred yards, we unknowingly drove into a bandits' nest. Men rushed out of the trees and blocked our car. The vehicle's windows were open and the men shouted, "Americans! Americans!" My heart raced, but it really started pounding after Peter calmly said, "Oh boy." I looked up and noticed that the leader had drawn a loaded pistol and was pointing it at the driver's head in front of me.

I'd never been in a situation this life-threatening before, but I realized a truth I've heard from others: when potentially fatal danger comes, all you can do is pray. I prayed for our safety. I prayed for my life. I prayed for my family in case I got kidnapped and held for ransom. Or killed. *God, give my family strength if this doesn't go our way. Especially my mother. She worries so.*

The driver deliberated with the gunman, who clearly wanted to be paid but refused to negotiate a bribe because he thought it would come out of what we'd promised to pay him. He revved the engine, threatening to drive through the crowd of men. One of our guides begged him in Creole: "Please stop. Negotiate. We'll pay them."

Our hired driver negotiated a bribe. Apparently, in Haiti it is a big no-no not to share. The men were upset that the driver, a man who lived in their community, was making money and not sharing with others. They only wanted the amount he was receiving.

Fumbling through our cash, we paid the leader and he waved us through. The other men continued shouting, not happy that he had not negotiated a higher rate. As our Land Cruiser drove off, I put my head in my lap in case one of them shot out our back window. When I rose moments later, we were safely back on the highway and on our way.

Later that evening in Port-au-Prince, I was still shaken, but we needed to exchange our remaining cash for local currency so we could pay the airport fees to leave the country. We left our hostel in search of a bank, but we were cornered by another group of men, who robbed us again. In one day, I'd been robbed twice, nearly kidnapped by armed bandits, and was nursing rumbles from an empty belly.

A cursory reading of Haitian history reveals that its problems didn't begin with an earthquake. They've been riddled with difficulty—government corruption, slavery, revolt, oppression, extreme poverty, violence, coups, floods, and foreign occupation alternating with foreign neglect. As Pooja Bhatia of the *New York Times* lamented, "If God exists, he's really got it in for Haiti."[3]

Bhatia echoes the sentiments of the Haitians themselves. Well known for their homespun proverbs, you might often hear a Haitian speak a phrase in Creole that translates, "Behind the mountain is another mountain." In America, a similar phrase might be, "When it rains it pours." The people of this small country have begun to feel as if their troubles may never end. In my short time there, I'd witnessed the handiwork of the one who comes to steal, kill, and destroy. His fingerprints were everywhere.

At first glance, Haiti can appear to be a most difficult country, mired in political and financial problems—a place that seems, well, impossible.

. . .

When you're in a place like Haiti, the natural human tendency is to throw up one's hands and condemn the whole house. *God could work a miracle in this situation,* we say, *but He probably won't. It's too messy, too broken, too rooted.* We prefer a ministry project a little closer to home, one where we can execute a foolproof plan and celebrate success on an ongoing basis. Who wants to toil over a place like Haiti for years and years when one can accomplish goals in a safer and more promising place? We are a hand-throwing people, but lucky for us, we serve a God who doesn't give up so easily.

If you read the Bible straight through, you'll find that God enjoys transforming impossible circumstances into places of great possibility. God causes barren wombs to open and suns to sit motionless in the sky. He turns shepherds into monarchs and dethrones the mightiest kings in a blink. And even more interesting are the people He uses to work these miracles. When God called Jeremiah, he said he was too young for the job. Moses argued that God should gather applications from better public speakers. But God likes to take impossible people and do impossible things.

"Nothing is impossible with God," the angel Gabriel said.[4] But do I really believe this or has it become a useful cliché I offer to those in dire circumstances?

As an overchurched youth growing up, I along with my friends often cited Philippians 4:13: "I can do all things through Christ." Many a Baptist boy and girl scribbled this passage in friends' yearbooks, claimed it as their "life verse," and when they were old enough, got it tattooed on their ankles. But we didn't believe it. We couldn't speak in tongues, and we couldn't get our virginities back. If there was even an ounce of sin in our lives, we believed we couldn't have a relationship with God. So no, not everything was possible for us, even when God was involved. Like many God followers, we claimed to serve the God of impossibility, but we confined Him so tightly, the belief could never be tested.

"Ah, Lord God! Behold, You have made the heavens and the earth by Your great power and by Your outstretched arm!" Jeremiah declared. "Nothing is too difficult for You."[5]

What task is too great for God? What hurdle can He not jump? What obstacle can He not overcome?

I may not be in circumstances as dire as most Haitians, but I still face seemingly impossible situations. And so do those around me. Sibling relationships broken beyond repair. Loved ones who aren't just estranged from God; they hate Him. Temptations and physical illness and nagging anxieties.

Some neighbors of mine recently had a "mountains beyond mountains" kind of year. They lost their jobs. Then their house. Then the pressure of it all began to gnaw at their marriage, sending them into a deep depression. As soon as they climbed to the apex of one cliff, their hearts sank as they found themselves facing another daunting peak.

The longer I follow Jesus, the more convinced I am that He wants to meet us in these kinds of circumstances, in life's seemingly impossible situations. When I set out to become a writer, it didn't make any sense. I had never published anything, not even a devotional in a church newsletter. I tested out of every college English course except an upper-level Civil War literature class that I took as an elective. My degree was in science.

"God, I believe You're leading me to do this," I said, "so I'm going to pray in that direction, trust You to equip me for the task, and work as hard as I can."

In that experience, I benefited from three disciplines:

Praying for the impossible. I claim to believe in a God who can and wants to work miracles, but my prayers rarely probe those places. I keep my requests limited to tasks I can well accomplish myself, perhaps because I'm afraid God won't come through. If I don't ask God to rescue me or heal my body, I don't have to worry about how to cope if He chooses not to. I often lament my weak faith, but should I expect more when my prayers are even weaker?

"You do not have because you do not ask God," the Bible reminds us.[6] I often wonder if one of the reasons I and many others I know witness so few miracles is due to the prayers we pray.

Trusting God for the impossible. For three years after I felt God's call on my life, it seemed like every newspaper, magazine, and book publisher in America rejected me. I questioned whether I'd really understood what God was trying to say to me. Or perhaps, I reasoned, it wasn't God's voice at all. Maybe it was all in my head. The most difficult step in meeting God in the impossible is believing He'll show up there. I've learned to pause in prayer and verbally acknowledge to God that I have complete confidence in Him. That I know He loves me, wants the best for me, and is working in my favor. To say this *and mean it* is one of the most difficult faith acts a person can take.

The Bible is chock-full of men and women who not only prayed seemingly impossible prayers, but also believed God would come through. In a mysterious way, one's faith in the request is as important as the request itself. When I give in to unbelief, I'm voting God off the island. But when I shift to a posture of faith I'm agreeing with God that new possibilities exist.

When Jesus first revealed to His friends and neighbors in Nazareth that He was more than the boy they once knew, they couldn't wrap their minds around it. "Wait a minute," one person objected. "This is Joseph's son. I remember when He was no bigger than a grasshopper. His sister lives two houses down from me. He's a carpenter, not a world changer."[7] The Scripture tells us that Jesus was astonished at their lack of faith.[8] Their faithlessness grew into frustration, which morphed into fury. While they were arguing over which one of them should toss Jesus over the cliff, He passed through their midst and went His way.[9]

I often wonder what kinds of miracles Jesus would have worked in Nazareth if they had believed the impossible. If they could have wrapped their minds around a Messiah who played games with their children, would Nazareth's blind have glimpsed their friends' faces? Would their lame have danced? In the same way, when I am not daring to believe God for the impossible, am I missing out on miracles?

Joining God in the impossible. Once I pray and believe, I can't sit back, arms folded, waiting for the stars to align. I have to join God in the seemingly impossible places like Haiti, believing He'll work. The apostle James said that believing in the impossible without actively doing something is dead faith. Not even a fully charged defibrillator can resuscitate it. Acting and behaving must follow asking and believing.

I think of Peter, that stubborn bloke who frustrated Jesus to the point of love. He was standing on the edge of the boat with the wind pressing against his cheekbones. In the distance he could see Jesus standing atop Galilee as if it were made of wooden planks.

"Come," Jesus said.

Peter immediately slung one leg over. Then another. He didn't stop to take a course in physics or ask Jesus to let him practice first in more shallow waters. He just stepped into impossibility, trusting that his Master would meet him there. If you've ever stepped onto a skateboard for the first time—trusting your safety to the shaky platform that seems poised to lay you on your back—you know how Peter may have felt. You may stumble or fall along the way—Peter did too—but the risk of stepping out is worth it and the result will be too.

I remember the night I got an e-mail from an editor telling me my first article had been accepted for publication. Two years and eight months had passed since I'd first felt God's nudge to begin this life path, and the rejections had begun to cripple my confidence. As soon as I realized what happened, I ran around my apartment screaming and leaping. I was elated, and I was relieved. But I would never have realized this dream without prayer, trust, and a decision to begin honing the craft of writing and pitching article ideas. I had to step out of the boat and learn to walk on the water that lay before me. The experience taught me that though God doesn't need us to do the work for Him, He takes pleasure in working through us to accomplish His plans.

At the same time, these disciplines do not come with a money-back guarantee. In the years since my first article was published, I've realized that God will not enter every circumstance and work a miracle like I expect Him to. Though God *can* do all things, He chooses not to do some of them. Sometimes the ocean doesn't part, and the womb remains barren. The earth keeps spinning, and the sun sets. The cancer metastasizes, and the sibling refuses the invitation for reconciliation.

Believing in a God of the impossible is not the same as having a heavenly bellhop who always services my needs on my timetable and according to my specifications. Rather, it means deciding to live in a posture that makes space for God to show up. It means believing that faith matters and prayers make a difference. And it means accepting that sometimes my prayers and actions are going to achieve the impossible in other times and places, unknown to me on this side of eternity.

* * *

Being held at gunpoint by bandits wasn't the most memorable part of my trip to Haiti. Not by a long shot. A few hours outside of Port-au-Prince, HOPE had several "savings circles," or community cooperatives where groups of individuals pool their money to make low-interest loans and save for essential purchases or start businesses. Each group elects a president, vice president, secretary, and treasurer to help oversee the process.

In Haiti, when they bury the dead, the last step is to crack the coffin door so grave robbers won't dig it up and resell it. In such a context, any extra money left after one pays the bills has a way of vanishing. The needs of others in the community tug at every spare penny. Savings circles provide intercommunity accountability for how money is stewarded.

A fifteen-year-old boy told me through a toothy grin that he was saving to go to college and become a doctor one day. A middle-aged woman told me that she'd saved up over the last year to buy a pig and a new door for her house. In the coming year, she plans to use the money to add on to their family's home. And perhaps most memorable, one portly man said, "Before I joined this group, my extra money passed through my stomach. Now I'm saving it and making a better life for my children."

In addition to the economic value, there are social and spiritual benefits. Social circles provide a network of encouragement. If members are discouraged, the others work to lift their spirits. When a member is sick, the others visit. In one group, I heard a story about a member's mother who passed away, and the group used some of their interest earnings to support the family. One woman said she's learned about transparency and honesty. Another that he has learned to support his friends and put God first.

After darkness settled one evening, Peter and I visited a savings circle meeting in a rectangular church that lacked electricity. The group sat in the first pews, and facing them, the treasurer tallied the week's deposits. A young boy held a flashlight over the treasurer's shoulder. This seemed a metaphor for what community cooperation was becoming in this country—a beam of light in a sea of darkness.

When the meeting concluded, I chatted with a few of the members.

One man handed me a business card for Salem Tires with bold letters: VITAL ALEXANDER, MANAGER.

"That's me," he said, grinning wide.

Another man named Derek told me that he used to be a beggar, and felt that everyone looked down on him. Today, he rides a bike to a business he owns. When people look at him now, he says, their eyes are different. Like Vital's, Derek's posture is no longer head down and palms up, but rather shoulders back and chin up.

Peter believes community and economic development programs like HOPE's can help eliminate extreme poverty from the face of the earth. Unlike charity programs, these solutions offer people dignity, responsibility, and ownership. In Haiti, many people have passions and gifts that go unused, but HOPE empowers them to put their God-given talents to work.

"Christians often patronize people we hope to minister to by telling them that we can do for them because they are incapable of doing themselves," Peter says. "Instead, HOPE works to remind them that they *can* do the things they believed they were incapable of."

Turn on your television or visit a news site and you may hear stories of Haiti—most of them negative and many full of stereotypes. But this island nation is brimming with other kinds of stories. Tales of hope and redemption, reconciliation and progress. People who didn't have jobs are now gainfully employed. Those who had forgotten how to dream are relearning. Broken relationships are being mended. And the Body of Christ is being built up.

The chasm between a hopeless Haiti and one where dreams are birthed seems wide. As do the gulches between a troubled marriage and a happy one, a fractured relationship and a harmonious one, a calling sensed and one realized.

· · ·

To begin bridging these gaps in my life, I've had to start nurturing a spiritual imagination. In the religious tradition in which I was raised, I wasn't encouraged to engage my imagination in the walk of faith. Scripture memory? Yes. The construction of tightly reasoned apologetic arguments? Of course. But imagination was not a necessary discipline. For me, rational thought was idolized, and imagination was a box of toys marked CHILDREN ONLY. Kids instinctively and regularly engaged theirs, but by adolescence they began weaning off the stuff.

By adulthood, parents have lost the imaginations they see bursting out of their own kids. Adults think pillows were made for sleeping, but children know they can become forts and bunkers. They see sticks as army guns and seashells as Frisbees. A child's world is packed with endless, imaginative possibilities, which may begin to explain why Jesus said that before someone can enter the kingdom of heaven they must "change and become like little children."[10] How else can one visualize, much less participate in, a world where up is down, first is last, less is more, enemies are loved, giving beats receiving, the humbled are exalted, and leading means serving?

Following God is an imaginative exercise, which is to say it means living in a posture where I am always envisioning new realities that more closely align with the world God desires. "Faith," says theologian James Whitehead, "is the enduring ability to imagine life in a certain way."[11]

Following Jesus means learning to look not once but twice.[12] A woman with teased hair and a painted-on dress stands on the corner of Main Street and Third Avenue, and I think, *Prostitute.* I look again and see a mother reconciled with the children she's neglecting, working to rescue women from the sex industry. A man sleeps on the stairs of the downtown theater and I think, *Drunk.* A second look, and I see a man who's been sober for twenty years leading the Wednesday-night AA class at the local church. A teenager stands outside of the movie theater with a group of friends poking fun at a passerby, and I think, *Trouble-maker.* But then I look again, and see a man who volunteers at a home for troubled children.

For much of my life, I've let films and television and magazines and newscasters tell me what kind of world I live in. They tell me the world is harsh and dangerous, sometimes downright hope-less. They say it stinks of poverty and swells with malnourished kids—millions and millions of them. At every corner, someone waits to swindle you or cheat you or fool you into thinking a millionaire overseas has died and left you their estate, which you can claim with a minor up-front investment. The world is a great place to live, they tell me, but only if you're wealthy or famous or sneakier than everyone else.

But the Scriptures tell me of a different world. One where the God of the universe can be found hiding out in the lowly places, crouched next to a makeshift fire in a slum, waiting to work miracles. It tells me of a God who loves a challenge and who never fails to notice the evils we hear so much about. The world the Bible describes is full of new possibilities, wrought by God's power, that can cure blindness, heal wounds, and feed us with next to nothing. This world is inhabited by a community of God's people, who've been empowered by the Holy Spirit of the Most High God to turn over the tables of injustice and oppression, if only they are willing to see the world through the lens of the kingdom and work together when the Spirit says, Go. But we will never see this world if we aren't looking for it.

"Consider the fig tree," Jesus says. "Look at the sheep in your pen and the coin in your pocket. Take note of the farmers and fishermen. Nothing is as it seems." Jesus used these images and stories to teach people in order to ignite their imaginations, because, He says, humans left to themselves will hear without understanding and see without perceiving.

I often choose to live with my fingers in my ears and my hands over my eyes. But if I could begin to look and listen, Jesus says, I would open a supernatural door to my heart and open the windows of possibility.[13]

As I learn to look twice rather than once, the world shifts before my eyes. Where once I only saw limitations and guardrails, with Christ, the boundaries are ripped from the edges. Preconceptions become misconceptions.

One of my favorite childhood authors was E. B. White, who wrote such classics as *Charlotte's Web* and *Stuart Little*. In his essay "Home-Coming," White recalled a column by Bernard DeVoto from *Harper's Magazine* that mourned a recent trip to the Maine coast. The writer described the highway into Maine as "overpopulated and full of drive-ins, diners, souvenir stands, purulent amusement parks, and cheap-Jack restaurants." White was confused because he too had driven that route recently and had had a much different experience. He noticed many of the things DeVoto did, but also more. White recounted seeing birch and spruce trees, kingly deer and sly foxes. The difference?

White concluded, "Probably a man's destination colors the highway, enlarges or diminishes its defects. Gliding over the tar, I was on my way home. DeVoto, traveling the same route, was on his way to what he described rather warily as 'professional commitments,' by which he probably meant that he was on his way somewhere to make a speech or get a degree. Steering a car toward home is a very different experience from steering a car toward a rostrum, and if our findings differ, it is not that we differed greatly in powers of observation but that we were headed in different emotional directions."[14]

Where I'm going determines what I see, and what I see can affect my entire experience of living. Too often, I live life from one commitment to the next. No wonder the world seems so flat. When I begin to look again, to see the world as an ordained adventure en route to Christ's kingdom, everything looks different: my neighbors, my nephew, my vocation, and even my experiences in troubled places like Haiti.

God's kingdom is breaking through. To see it and enter it, I must become like a child: imagining a better world and praying for it, believing God for it, and stepping into it myself. The One who wants to show up and surprise me might just be waiting in the unlikely, the improbable, and, yes, the seemingly impossible.

5

A Thread Called Grace

Encountering Jesus in Honesty

"Hush, Dorothy," whispered the Tiger, *"you'll ruin my reputation if you are not more discreet. It isn't what we are, but what folks think we are, that counts in this world."*

—From L. Frank Baum's *The Road to Oz*

Have you ever had something in your life that you were afraid to say aloud to someone else? A struggle that you held beneath the surface and didn't want anyone to know about? A secret that you packed in a box and swore never to open? I've carried mine since childhood. And when I woke on July 26, 2012, I had no idea it would be exposed, not just to my family and friends, but posted online for the world to see.

As best I can remember, my secret began early when I was around the age of seven. That was how old I was when Michael, a much older boy who lived in a brick house near the front of our neighborhood, began to sexually abuse me.

Michael's family and mine had been friends for years. We were drawn together by his father's terminal cancer. My parents would look after Michael and his sister in the afternoons so his dad could rest after chemotherapy. We'd pick them up for church on the weekends so they wouldn't miss Sunday school. The bond between our families was tight and only grew tighter the day lung cancer finally stole Michael's father's life.

He'd still come by to play with me and my brothers in the months after the funeral, but his countenance was different—frustrated and pensive. He always seemed to be pondering something but never voiced what vexed him. One evening when Michael was spending the night in my room, he told me that boys could have secret kinds of fun without parents noticing. As he spoke, he put his hands in places never touched except by undergarments, and my body froze in fear and confusion.

Later, I grew anxious about what happened.

"Can a boy get AIDS just from touching a private part?" I asked my parents.

They told me no, but when they asked me why I was inquiring, I changed the subject. I was too scared to tell them what happened—indeed, too paralyzed by fear to tell anyone. I should just forget about it and move on, I supposed. But I couldn't move on, for it would happen again, this time while I was playing a video game in Michael's bedroom. And then again, after he checked to make sure no one was around and pushed me into an upstairs linen closet.

I can't tell you how many times something like this occurred. I remember those three vividly and when I let my mind wander, I can still see the events in my mind like I'm watching an old 8mm film. I guess it doesn't matter how many times it happened, only that it did. And it singed a part of my soul in a way I can't explain. Now it only hurts when I press down on the injury, but at the time, I lived with a dull throb and occasional shooting pains.

With my parents and brothers, school counselors and friends, I never let on that anything was wrong. But it was. For something inside of me had been bruised. Or broken. The best way to let it heal, I determined, was to deal with it myself.

No one can help me.

No one can protect me.

No one can fix what hurts.

I. Am. On. My. Own.

With that thought, I crammed all the pain and emotions and memories into a box. I tossed the box into a bag and wrapped the bag in duct tape and rolled the whole wad with a steel chain. On this chain, I clamped a lock whose key had been thrown away. And I buried it in my memory.

This is going to be my secret and now no one ever has to know.

With that, I believed I'd laid hold of safety and security and normalcy. No one knowing about my trauma seemed the second-best option to never having experienced it at all. For a moment, I felt the freedom to forget and exhale. But the liberty would not last.

When I was about ten years old, the isolation of my pain almost killed me as thoughts of suicide plagued my mind. I was so suffocated by my secret that I believed only death would provide me the space needed to breathe freely. One day, I remember walking into my room, locking my door, tying a brown leather belt around my frail neck, and trying to hang myself from my bedpost. It never occurred to me that the attempt was futile because I was taller than the wooden column.

As I contemplated how I could exit this world quickly and with the least amount of pain, I sat down and penned a three-page letter to my family. I shook with emotion and muffled my sobs as I shared everything I'd wrestled with and all the things I wanted to say but never mustered up the strength to speak. When finished, I placed the drenched pages into a small white envelope and taped it to the bottom of one of my dresser drawers. *If I ever get up the courage, I'll kill myself. But at least in death, they'll truly know me.* The letter remained in place for months, but eventually it became a source of fear and anxiety. *What if my mom stumbles across it while cleaning my room? I'll be committed to a mental institution.* When the pressure was too much, I retrieved the letter and tore it up.

The next few years of my life seemed to go well. I was an above-average student and happy enough—often quiet and yet humorous, like a reincarnated Harpo Marx. Friends were often difficult to come by, but I never blamed myself. I started to gain a little traction, and then middle school arrived. These years are awkward even for children with the most pristine pasts. Your face flares up with acne, kids discover how to be extra cruel, and your body begins to change with the influx of adolescent hormones. For me, this spelled trouble.

I felt attracted to pretty girls, though none of them gave me much attention. But I also felt myself drawn to other boys. I stuffed these in my mind's box, never to be shared. After all, I was the son of a prominent evangelical pastor, and I knew that if anyone found out, I'd be dodging stares and whispers in the supermarket. That's the last thing I wanted.

In high school, I had several healthy relationships with girls, but I was still insecure beneath the façade of confidence. And in college, I rigorously devoted myself to my studies, embracing it as a welcome escape. I dated a few girls from time to time, but the turmoil inside kept me from letting myself get too close to anyone. I didn't feel like much of a man, and even when I was attracted to a girl, I was afraid I would never be able to love her as I wanted to.

I've been asked what kind of connection I see between these adolescent feelings and the childhood abuse I experienced. Did the childhood abuse shape my adolescent and young-adult experiences, or were those parts of me already there? I'm certain I don't know the answer to this question, and I'm not sure anyone does except God.

By 2009, my writing career was in full swing. I was entering my late twenties and enjoying much success. I wrote an opinion column for *USA Today* titled "An Evangelical's Plea: 'Love the Sinner.'"

"One of the mantras of evangelicalism over the past quarter-century regarding gay men and lesbians has been 'Hate the sin, love the sinner,'" I wrote. "If, however, you google the public statements made by evangelicals regarding our gay neighbors, you'll uncover a virtual how-to manual on hating sin and little if anything about loving sinners."[1]

I asked readers to do away with self-gratifying monologues and harsh language. I pled with Christians to abandon clichés such as the infamous "God made Adam and Eve, not Adam and Steve."

"Now is the time for those who bear the name of Jesus Christ to stop merely talking about love and start showing love to our gay and lesbian neighbors," I concluded. "It must be concrete and tangible. It must move beyond cheap rhetoric. We cannot pick and choose which neighbors we will love. We must love them all."[2]

Though no one knew, the article was written with my secret lockbox in view. I was not just asking that we do a better job loving our neighbors; I wanted to know I too was loved.

In response to the article, I was contacted by a gay blogger who wanted to dialogue more about my article. Over many months, we communicated by e-mail and texts. I began to grow comfortable with him, and finally, I shared my story of struggle with him.

When I was traveling through a city near him, we met for dinner, and as we were saying good-bye, we had physical contact that fell short of sex but went beyond the bounds of friendship. Afterward, I went back to my hotel room by myself and lay there, sorting through my clouded emotions.

Alone.

*   *   *

He and I ceased communication soon after, and I never saw him again, but years later, the day I feared finally arrived. I woke to prepare a talk I was giving at a local church on the subject of grace. The sermon centered on a solitary question: *How do you forgive the unforgivable?* With my coffeemaker gurgling in the background, I had no idea the answers I'd come up with were ones I'd need mere moments later.

I decided to check my e-mail. The sender line read "Google Alert," and the article linked to was written by the blogger I'd met for dinner. Though he hadn't shared every detail, he was threatening to.

I fell to my knees next to my kitchen table with tears in the corners of my eyes: "Lord, I can't do this. I'm not ready. I'm not strong enough."

My heart heard the reply: "It's time."

I sat in silence for a bit—five, maybe ten minutes—and my cell phone rang. A friend was calling to tell me he'd seen the same story, but not from the original post. A Christian blogger had already picked up the story. There was no going back.

The following days tasted bitter, and I got a lot of unhelpful advice. One friend told me to "throw the gay community under the bus and save yourself." Another, who was a high-powered publicist, said I should kill the story by digging up garbage on the blogger who wrote the post. But I couldn't shake Jesus's words that those who live by the sword die by it also. Those who survive by destroying others will themselves be destroyed. My platform as a writer allowed me an opportunity to test that maxim, but I chose a different response.

Rather than attack or defend, I opted for honesty. I shared my story through an interview on a good friend's Web site:

> Although I was unable to choose when I would share some of these painful memories, I am thankful for the opportunity to share it now. I'm thankful that I am able to make better decisions about how to handle a difficult situation. And I'm thankful that because of grace,

I can identify with those who have dealt with similar situations.

It's bred compassion in me toward others who wrestle with the baggage they carry in life. People like me who passionately pursue God—on His terms and not ours—experience incredible times of struggle along the way. I know what it is like to experience periods of depression, frustration, and confusion. And that's why I live out my calling the way I do, as best as I can, sometimes stumbling along the way.

Every keystroke was a struggle, but the words I heard that fateful morning rang in my ears: *It's time.*

My deepest, darkest secrets were now on display for the world to read. I knew that I might live with this for the rest of my life. But the lock on my box had been shattered, and I was already beginning to feel liberated from its captivity.

.   .   .

Being raised in a pastor's home, I am acutely aware of what everyone else thinks about me. I notice the looks, monitor the whispers, and manage the perceptions. Growing up, we sometimes had fights while riding to church in our family minivan with my parents and two brothers. This is a common scenario for most families, but ours always had the same ending. When we arrived at church, Mom or Dad would turn around and say, "Okay. We're at church now. Time for everyone to be on their best behavior. You're Merritts. You need to act like it."

The door slid open and a transformation occurred. When we stepped out, smiles had replaced scowls. We'd hold hands even though we really wanted to pull each other's arms out of socket. The tone of our voices changed from scathing to saccharine. And as years of this behavior progressed, I became skilled in wearing a mask.

"I heard the sound of You coming in the garden, and I was afraid because I am naked," Adam told God in Genesis, "so I hid."[3] The human inclination is to conceal when we feel naked or exposed or vulnerable. I wanted to hide from the pain of sexual abuse and the confusion I felt, so my mask rarely came off. I lived behind it.

Hiding behind my disguise was crushing and conflicting because at my core—at everyone's core—is a desire to be fully known. I want others to see me, both the beautiful and wretched parts. And often my desire to be known is almost as strong as my fear of being known.

I fashioned my mask because I believed, in the words of Parker Palmer, "[my] inner light will be extinguished or [my] inner darkness will be exposed."[4] My secret was intended to shield me from experiencing more pain, but it only isolated me from those with whom I needed to share my true self. I became more a performer and less of a person.

"I not only have my secrets, I *am* my secrets. And you are yours," Frederick Buechner said. "Our secrets are human secrets, and our trusting each other enough to share them with each other has much to do with the secret of what it means to be human."[5]

The months after my story was posted online were some of the most humanizing of my life. One night after a particularly difficult day, I turned into my neighborhood to see cars lined up along the curb outside of my house. A group of my friends waited in the driveway. When I pulled in, they said they'd come to pray with me and over me. I hadn't been home when they'd arrived an hour earlier, so they'd decided to wait. I choked back tears and welcomed them in.

I sat cross-legged on the floor of my living room and my friends surrounded me, laying their hands on my back and shoulders, grasping my arms. One by one, they prayed for grace and mercy and strength and divine presence. Hot tears fell off their cheeks and landed on my neck and arms, mingling with mine as they ran down.[6]

That evening, I became more "me" than I'd ever been. For once, I wasn't trying to burnish my surface, to create an alternate version of myself that was more acceptable or likable. I was finally able to lower my shoulder, drop my mask, and just exist in the present moment.

I found comfort in the Old Testament story of Jacob. In Genesis 27, where we meet him, his first words are, "I am Esau." With his eyes set on blessings and inheritance, Jacob finds himself captured by the desire to be someone else. He wants to be the better one, the brawnier one, the beloved one, the firstborn. Jacob wants to be Esau.

As time unfurls, Jacob learns to live in pursuit of God and a transformation happens. In Genesis 32, he is asked, "What is your name?" to which he replies, "It is Jacob." Modern Americans can easily miss this because our names don't have quite the significance they did in that time. Whether one is named Rosalyn or

Zoey, Josh or Gregory, makes very little difference. "Don't judge a book by its cover," we might say. "It's the inside that counts."

But the ancients were worlds apart from us on the importance of names. Ancient names describe who a person is and what marks them as individuals. Isaac means "laughter," Abimelech means "my father is king," and the prophet Isaiah called his first son Shear-Jashub, or "a remnant shall return." Moses means "to draw out." The name was given because his mother drew him out of a river, but God had something bigger in mind.

God displays the importance of a name when He says to Abraham, "I am El Shaddai."[7] It was quite a gift for Abraham to receive the divine name, which Jews today will not even speak or write out of respect. Later, when Moses questioned whether he was up to the task God was giving him, El Shaddai would tell him, "I AM WHO I AM. This is what you say to the Israelites, 'I AM has sent me to you.' . . . This is my name forever, the name you shall call me from generation to generation."[8] By giving His name, God offered more than a way to identify Him; God gave them an ancient and intimate invitation into relationship.

For this reason, Jesus shocked the crowds when He proclaimed, "Before Abraham was born, I AM!"[9] More than a statement of His role as God's son and messenger, Jesus was telling them that the intimate relationship that God offered their ancestors could be accessed through Christ. And the sign of this relationship is not a signed contract or a firm handshake, but a name.

Names mattered, and when one was changed, it was more than a legal matter to be taken care of at the county courthouse. It signaled a shift in the individual's identity. God changed Abram and Sarai's names to Abraham ("father of a multitude") and Sarah ("queen") as a reminder of His promise to make them the parents of a great nation. Jesus changed Simon's name to Peter as an expression of his future role in forming the Church.

So this subtle shift we see in Jacob's life turns out to be significant. The closer God drew Jacob in, the more comfortable Jacob became with who he is—both the smooth spots and the rough edges. He is ready to be fully used because he is ready to be honest about who he has been and who God has created him to be. As he learns to trust God, he learns to be honest with the story in which he is intertwined like strands of cord. And as I learn to lean into God, I am able to make similar shifts.

This is part of what Jesus was getting at when He said, "Peace I leave with you; my peace I give to you."[10] Because the English word "peace" comes from the Latin word *pax*, we assume it means the absence of conflict, a time in which wars have ceased. But the Hebrew concept of peace or *shalom* means much more than that. It literally translates "wholeness," and it means having everything you need to be fully and wholly who God has created you to be.[11] *Shalom* is the "hope that we experience physical, emotional and psychological peace, that we do not experience any disturbance to our bodies, our hearts or our minds."[12]

This is what Jesus offers—an opportunity to set myself free by understanding who I am in the context of who God is and what God wants for me.

But if trading secrets for honesty is so liberating, then why is it so difficult? In my case and many others, it is because of shame.

Secrets draw their power from shame. I convince myself that I am too messed up, too tainted, or too tarnished for others to accept. Or maybe people will think I am a fraud. As I believe these lies, shame grows into fear, which is almost always, at some level, fear that if others truly know me, they won't love me. Or at least love me as much or in the same way.

In order to release my secrets, I must uncurl my white-knuckled fingers from deep desires:

- My desire to be perfect
- My desire to be liked
- My desire to be in control
- My desire to be successful

Without releasing these desires, my shame will keep my secrets locked up and convince me they can never be disclosed. It forces me to forge masks for myself and hide under them. Whether one faces an eating disorder, a marriage failure, insecurities and inadequacies, or just something done that they don't feel free enough to share with others, shame can trap us in the mire of our secrets and steal from us the gift of openness with those we love.

"Shame keeps us from telling our own stories and prevents us from listening to others tell their stories," says Brené Brown, "We silence our voices and keep our secrets out of the fear of disconnection."[13] In the end, shame steals the very thing it promises: meaningful, authentic connections with others. Pursuing a life of honesty means to reveal who I truly am and assert that my story too belongs at the table.

As I took off my mask and wept with my friends that evening, I sensed there was an unseen guest in my midst. In the swirling cocktail of healing, grief, shared love, compassion, and prayer, God was present. Standing. Observing. And maybe even cheering.

*　*　*

As the furor died down, reality set in and I realized that I'd be okay. In fact, I'd be better than okay. I took a month off to travel, rest, and reflect. As I opened these secret spaces and invited God in, He rushed in like a flash flood. He reminded me that He has me *even in this* and offered me the very things I convinced myself I'd never attain. He bathed me with grace and mercy and provision, proving again that He can be trusted with those sore and sensitive places, and working miracles in my midst.

My friend Marilyn approached me recently with wet eyes. She'd shared my story with her sister, who in turn told her about a period of abuse perpetrated by their uncle. Somehow my story became one of the keys that unlocked the box in her life. The unspoken wedge that once divided Marilyn from her sister has now been removed, and healing is happening.

A woman named Crystal was one of more than a hundred who sent me an e-mail in recent months. She was raised by a single mother and abused by a neighbor who she thought was a friend. She didn't tell anyone what happened, but the ripples from the trauma flooded her life. "I now feel free enough to share my story," she wrote at the close of her note.

God was setting me free by calling me to a place of honesty. And through my liberation, He was freeing others as well. When the storm swept through my life, I didn't know what in the world God was up to. Or if He was even involved. But the storm helped me see God in ways I'd never imagined. As it turns out, sometimes God lets our house burn down so we can better see the sun rise.

Though I'm still on this journey toward honesty, I can't help but marvel at what God has accomplished. When I consider the freedom I now feel, I praise Him. When I see others finding freedom, I rejoice yet again. God's mercies really are new each morning.

A woman in my church walked up not long ago and said, "I feel so bad for you. Your wounds are so deep." I appreciated her concern, but I also felt she didn't have the whole story.

"It's okay, ma'am," I replied. "I *am* wounded, and while I have deep holes in my heart, they are not empty. They are filled with grace."

Honesty has a way of humbling us, and it has me. It has softened my heart. As I've been honest about the bruised and broken parts of myself, the openness has become a doorway for God's healing.

For weeks after being "outed," I slept like a baby, and by that I mean I was up all night crying. But over time, the pain dulled and God started working. I'd stopped worrying about perfect performance and shaping others' perceptions of me. I drew close to God's embrace, and we conversed with a frankness we'd never shared.

After my moment of honesty, I spent two weeks with a counselor in the Rocky Mountains talking through events and feelings I'd never spoken out loud. There I realized that the ultimate key to move from secrecy to honesty is not telling the whole world, but rather letting God have access, giving Him permission to speak into the dusty recesses of the hidden places, and letting Him become a conversation partner as I sorted through the rubble.

In a celebrity age, everyone feels they have a right to know about every intimate detail of everyone else's life. If people find you have a secret, they often assume that you should divulge every chapter and verse to the entire world. But often the ones who demand to know the most deserve to know the least. I learned from this experience that the way to move from secrecy to honesty isn't to share every detail of my life with anyone who demands an answer. Instead, it requires opening the lockbox I've tucked away and dumping the contents at the Lord's feet. To discover the authentic life, I invite God into the secret spaces to fill them with grace.

When people today ask me how I identify myself, I never quite know how to answer. It doesn't feel authentic to label the whole of my being by feelings and attractions, and my experience has been that those parts of me tend to be somewhat fluid. One day I may feel more one way than another, and the next I feel a little differently. I am far more than my feelings, so I don't answer that question. Not because I want to evade others but because I want to stay true to myself.

The essence of who I am is far more shaped, influenced, and guided by my spirituality than by my sexuality. I am wholly wrapped up in my pursuit of Christ and His amazing grace. And

I'm quite comfortable there. When I'm feeling pretty bad about myself, when the wounds of my heart cry out loud for healing, when shame attempts to suffocate me, or when I'm especially discouraged over my most tragic failures, I find myself holding onto a thread. A thread called grace.

6

Dying to Live

Encountering Jesus in Waiting

Where others see but the dawn coming over the hill, I see the sons of God shouting for joy.

— WILLIAM BLAKE

'm glad to see you above ground," the surgeon said to Carl as his eyes opened and came into focus. "You should be on the other side of the dirt."

Earlier that day, the surgeon had admitted Carl to perform a heart ablation, which is an invasive procedure used to remove a faulty electrical pathway in patients with irregular heartbeats. But during the operation, the surgeon's tool punctured a hole in the wall of Carl's heart. A thoracic surgeon was immediately called in to cut him open, and when he did, blood spurted out and painted the surgical team in warm red liquid. The doctor thrust his hand into the opening in Carl's chest and placed his finger in the hole to stop the bleeding.

With the loss of blood and trauma to his heart, Carl died on the table several times and was in a state of ongoing resuscitation, shocking him back to life. Because he was unconscious, Carl was not aware of the chaos in the room. But he remembers something vividly. He became aware of his body rising off the table and standing in a beautiful garden with the sun rising in the distance.

"It was just beautiful," he told me later as he stared out the window and fought back tears. "I had perfect peace. It was like I was surrounded by the presence of God."

But Carl did not enjoy the sense of calmness long. He was thrust back to life and woke to a panicked wife, Jocelyn, standing over his weak body. She was concerned and unsure about what the future held for her husband of forty-eight years.

"Mrs. Russel," the attending nurse said, "you don't have to worry about Carl. I won't leave his side tonight."

With those words, Jocelyn felt she could return to the waiting room for some much needed shut-eye. As his wife left, the nurse bent over and whispered in his ear: "Don't worry. You're going to make it. There's a whole room of people praying for you. And I will be here with you."

Her words seemed to settle Carl's spirit, even though he knew the troubles weren't totally behind him. He had lost all of his own blood during the procedure, as well as his hearing in his left ear. Worse still, his heart had been seriously damaged.

Heart problems aren't new to Carl. His father had serious cardiological complications, and two of his uncles had died before age fifty from heart attacks. Carl himself struggled for years with an enlarged heart, two leaking valves, a pacemaker, and an irregular heartbeat. But after the botched ablation, his ticker was only functioning at around 15 to 20 percent. The situation was more dire than it had ever been.

In the months following, his condition worsened and testing showed that he was officially in congestive heart failure. The cardiologist announced: "You need a new heart."

After extensive evaluation, Carl was placed on the B-list and is waiting to make it onto the A-list from which most organ recipients are chosen. He is eligible for a heart transplant for only two more years. When he reaches seventy, he'll be taken off the list.

Carl struggles with the thought that someone has to die in order for him to live. And he wrestles with his less active life. He can't ride his bike or teach pitching lessons or pick up anything weighing more than five pounds. This is especially difficult for a lifelong athlete who played professional baseball with the Boston Red Sox organization for seven years. The patient whom doctors call "the miracle man" is having to embrace a slower pace and is limited in where he can travel, having to stay within three hours of the hospital at all times.

All he can do is wait.

* * *

As I spoke to Carl, I found myself wrapped up in his story. I too felt like I'd been in a waiting period. After crying out to God in my moment of emptiness, I had no other choice but to wait on Him to show up. In some ways, I felt like I too was waiting on a new heart. Or at least waiting for my old one to come back to life.

Existing in this period was torturous. As my friends can attest, I'm impatient by nature. I nearly leap out of my skin when I'm forced into a long checkout line at the grocery store, and I often catch myself responding to e-mails in the middle of one-on-one conversations. The two places I least want to be stuck are the Department of Motor Vehicles and hell. But, alas, I repeat myself.

Waiting is that excruciating place between where I am and where I want to go. I don't know when or how I developed this perspective. As a kid, I would fidget in church during sermons, trying to catch a glance at my mother's watch when she turned her wrist. When I reached sixteen and began to drive, sometimes I would check to make sure the coast was clear before running a red light. I couldn't bear the thought of waiting for it to turn green. These days, I often send an abbreviated text message to a friend or colleague because an e-mail would take too long.

Times have changed, rapidly increasing in pace, and the world around me waits for nothing. This physical reality has shaped my spirituality, which is why I want God to answer my prayers as soon as the request leaves my lips.

I grow weary in waiting because I think every wait is a waste. I'm wasting time, wasting energy, or wasting my day when I could be doing something more productive. Perhaps God sees these periods differently than I do. Maybe these times in life when I think I'm waiting, God is working. He's forming me, shaping me, preparing me for the destiny He's marked out for me.

This was true with God's servant Noah. When he was young, he sat around the campfire with his father, Lamech, and his 369-year-old great-granddaddy Methuselah. As firelight danced off their cheekbones, Noah would listen to them tell old family stories, but his favorite was the one about great-great-grandpa Enoch. Legend had it that Enoch was so righteous and favored by God that the Almighty finally seized him from the earth.[1]

"I want to walk with God like Enoch did," Noah would say to himself.

And one day, he would get his chance. But not before waiting 480 years. We don't know much about how Noah spent those five centuries, except that like his ancestor Enoch, "he found favor in the eyes of the Lord...Noah was a righteous man, blameless among the people of his time, and he walked with God."[2] For Noah, waiting on the Lord was an opportunity to walk with the Lord.

When he was almost half a millennium old, God came to him with some mixed news. The world had gone to pot, and the wickedness of humans was so great that God regretted creating them. He decided to wipe the slate clean and start over. But Noah would be spared, God said, if he performed one simple task: build a boat. I suspect Noah thought back to Enoch in that moment, because he didn't flinch an inch at God's request to construct an ark half the size of the *Titanic*. He just started building.

The Bible says that the first pitter-patter of rain was heard when Noah was six hundred years old.[3] God waited 120 years after His instructions to Noah, but scholars believe the construction project took a maximum of about seventy-five years. Why make Noah wait an extra forty-five years? Why allow him to endure the sneers and jeers of all the doubters and haters? Why not flood the earth the moment the last nail was driven in the last plank?

I can't say for sure, but I have a hunch that God was using the half century to prepare Noah for the coming catastrophe. When the fountains of the deep ruptured and the clouds began to weep, I can only imagine what Noah was experiencing inside that ark. Maybe he heard the muffled voices of childhood playmates or the pounding fist of his pregnant neighbor begging him to open the door.

Once the storm begins, God makes him wait again, this time for forty days and nights inside the cramped vessel until the rain stops pouring. He almost loses his mind as he rushes around— feeding, cleaning, muttering prayers. A few days in, he started to feel claustrophobic, but he stays beneath the deck to avoid the sight and stench of waterlogged animals floating by. After a month and a half of seasickness and clinging to God like a life preserver, Noah finds dry land and emerges from the watery wasteland. God promises never to send another flood like that again. He offers a rainbow as a reminder and says that He'll remember His words every time He sees it, and Noah trusts that God will always look in the right direction.[4]

Though the tale of Noah's flood is often romanticized, it is no childhood fable. Noah faced an event so mentally and emotionally traumatic that the world's best counselor would be of no use. Why did God make Noah wait another forty-five years before sending rain? I think He was preparing the gray-bearded geezer for what he would one day face.

As I look back on my life, I recognize that God often makes preparations *before* I need them. The words that lift me out of depression were often planted in childhood. Friendships that sustain me when I'm exhausted by life were formed years earlier. God continues to show me that when I'm waiting, He's working.

I suppose God does this because He is a good dad. A responsible parent sets aside money for a child's education early in life as he or she is able, not when college applications are submitted. Similarly, God uses times of waiting in my life to make provision for what He knows is coming.

And this is something of a divine pattern:

- God made Abraham and Sarah wait nearly one hundred years before the promised son was born. It took some time to prepare the old couple for parenthood.
- Joseph had to wait for years as a slave and prisoner before God promoted him to Pharaoh's palace and allowed him to face his backstabbing brothers. God knew that it takes time to say good-bye to bitterness.
- For forty years, Moses waited in the desert before God called him to rescue the Israelites. Apparently he had some kinks in his leadership style that needed to be worked out. Or perhaps God was getting him ready for another forty years of desert dwelling that God knew was in his future.
- After David was anointed king, God made him wait more than a decade to assume the throne. Shepherds don't become monarchs overnight.
- Paul, after his conversion, had to wait to start his ministry. Knowing the scourges, shipwrecks, and prisons that were in his future, God thought an Arabian vacation might be in order.

The Psalmist sang, "My soul waits in silence for God,"[5] and Isaiah said, "Those that wait on the Lord shall renew their strength."[6] The apostle James echoes a similar sentiment when he comments that God blesses those who wait.[7]

Even Jesus participates in the divine pattern of waiting. Jesus makes God's people wait four hundred years after the last book of the Old Testament was penned before He comes. Once here, He makes them wait another thirty years before He begins His ministry. After the crucifixion, Jesus makes the disciples wait three days for the resurrection. Why not two days? Or one? After all, the disciples were soaking in grief and confusion during that time.

And once Jesus returns to them, He promises to send the Holy Spirit. But not immediately. "Do not leave Jerusalem," Jesus tells them, "but *wait* for the gift my Father promised."[8]

Periods of waiting are not passive, hands-in-pocket interims. Rather they are the times in life when God is preparing us for a spiritual upgrade. Maybe that's why He has made two millennia of His postmortem disciples wait for Him to return. Jesus knows that waiting doesn't mean wasting. It means God is working.

Because of my natural anxieties, this is a difficult truth for me to swallow. During those times when I seek but don't find and knock but don't receive an answer, I have to return to these Scriptures and recommit myself to the process God is pushing me through. In these moments, I have to remind myself that faith is not just about trusting God for the *what*, but also the *when* and *how*, and that God's calendar looks different from the one on my iPhone. Jesus is better than I imagined because when I am waiting, He is working to prepare me for the floods, olive branches, and resurrections that only He knows are coming.

●　　●　　●

The day after Carl's botched surgery, Jocelyn walked down to the nurses' station to thank the kind nurse who told them not to worry. She was told that there was no one working in the hospital by that name.

"I'm convinced God put an angel in Carl's room that night to stay with him and to comfort us," she told me. "It was just the first sign that God was going to be with us while we waited."

I've known Carl and Jocelyn for most of my life, and I've watched the situation unfold firsthand. The day we met to discuss his experience, he'd been on the waiting list for about eight months. A rubbery tube poked out of his sleeve where medicine was injected into his heart. He was weak but hopeful.

Carl tells me that this period of waiting has drawn him closer to God. For starters, it has humbled him.

"I've always been an independent person who hates to depend on others for anything," he tells me. "Now I have to ask people for help all the time, and I'm noticing how God places people in my life to walk with me on this journey."

The experience has also made Carl more grateful, opening his eyes to the breadcrumbs of blessing that God has sprinkled along his path.

"I don't take life for granted like I used to. Now I enjoy walking the dog and listening to the birds sing," he whispers from under his silver-swept hair. "I even enjoy the process of waking up every day."

Jocelyn has also drawn closer to God. A self-described "control freak," she has had to learn to let go: "I like to be in charge of everything, but I've learned that I can't do anything to change the situation."[9]

As they recognize God at work in their period of waiting, Jocelyn and Carl cling to Psalm 73:26: "My flesh and my heart may fail, but God is the strength of my heart and my portion forever."[10]

The prophet Jeremiah says that every person is a plant, but we get to choose which kind of plant we want to be. If I choose to trust in my efforts to control life, I become like a bush in the parched places of the desert: dry and brittle and lifeless. But if I choose to place my confidence in the Lord, I become like a tree planted by a stream whose roots stretch into the water with supple fruit dangling from its limbs.[11]

The image of a tree planted in riverfront real estate is a timely one for someone like me, who grows weary in waiting. But a tree is always waiting. That's all it knows how to do. And while the tree is waiting, the river is on the move. And so it is with God.

I've spent my life waiting, and I suspect the pattern won't shift any time soon. But I've changed along the way. I've been learning to stay planted and stretch my roots deep into the water of God's grace. It's a lesson that humans have been learning since the days of Noah. And if the old sailor were alive now, I think he would tell me to trust that God is still working. As it turns out, sometimes waiting isn't waiting at all.

7

The Last Lullaby

Encountering Jesus in Tragedy

Would we know that the major chords were sweet,
If there were no minor key?
Would the painter's work be fair to our eyes,
Without shade on land or sea?
Would we know the meaning of happiness,
Would we feel that the day was bright,
If we'd never known what it was to grieve,
Nor gazed on the dark of night?
Many men owe the grandeur of their lives to their
tremendous difficulties.

—CHARLES SPURGEON

As I gaze into the eyes of my newborn niece, I think, *It takes a mountain of courage to be human.* Life for her is as peaceful as it will ever be. She sleeps and eats and receives love in unending cycles, and her worst worry is that her heavy-hanging diaper may sit for a minute longer than it ought. Presley knows nothing about depression or death or disappointment or the kind of fear that induces paralysis.

But one day she will.

A proud and overly protective uncle, I want to shield her from all the hurts that come with life on planet earth. That's what love does, even though love knows it isn't possible. When she's a grade-schooler, I don't want Presley to receive a failing grade on a paper that the child next to her aces. I don't want her heart to deflate as she realizes that she isn't the smartest girl who's ever lived. When she's twelve or fourteen, love will strike her like a mallet on a gong. I don't want the reverberations of heartbreak to shatter her naïve romanticism. I want to guard my niece from the scariness of life, and I hope the worst tragedy she'll witness will come by watching the evening news. But who's to say? Years from now, bones will likely fracture and friends may betray her, and in the chaos of it all, Presley might wonder if the sticker she saw in the grocery-store checkout line is true after all: "Life sucks and then you die."

"God give her courage," I pray when I peer into her innocent eyes. "She may need it to survive this life."

If Presley doesn't believe in the harsh realities heading her way, I could tell her a story about my friend Mark. When we first met, Mark was a math teacher who'd just moved to Georgia after completing a master's degree at Louisiana State University. He had the personality you'd expect from a math teacher—matter-of-fact with a dry humor—but if you could land a punch line, his belly laugh would brighten the room.

A smile would plaster his face after he met Hannah in a church community group I led. She was sweet and tender, and her countenance was punctuated by what Howard Thurman called "quiet eyes." But she was also strong. A three-time cancer survivor who'd overcome Hodgkin's lymphoma in college, Hannah had undergone every kind of cancer treatment imaginable—from stem cell transplants to complicated diets implemented by specialists in alternative medicine.

In March 2010, they said their *I do*s. At the wedding, they danced to Dana Glover's "It's You (I Have Loved)," setting the tone for what seemed a storybook existence. But two years later, tragedy struck.

June was like soup, wet and hot as it always is in Georgia, and Mark and Hannah were working outside their home. They were restaining their deck and doing some heavy yard work. When Hannah complained of neck and back pain that night, they chalked it up to sore muscles from the day's labor. The pain increased along with her temperature. When the fever reached 103 degrees, Hannah lay in a cold bath to help drive it down. Mark, now worried, sang to her a Scottish lullaby that she loved—"Skye Boat Song":

Loud the winds howl, loud the waves roar,
Thunderclaps rend the air,
Baffled our foes stand by the shore,
Follow they will not dare.

⚬∞⚬

Speed, bonnie boat, like a bird on the wing,
Onward, the sailors cry.
Carry the lad that's born to be king
Over the sea to Skye.

The next morning, Hannah's symptoms worsened. She already had an appointment scheduled that day for a routine checkup with her oncologist, and Mark drove her. By the time they arrived, Hannah was in extreme pain and disoriented. Mark carried her dizzy body into the office.

The physician ran a few tests and, after seeing the results, sent her to the emergency room. Hannah arrived around midnight and was told that she had sepsis—a state of whole-body inflammation due to a severe infection in the blood. The bacteria in Hannah's blood was commonly found in the saliva of dogs, and doctors believed her one-year-old puppy had infected her. The word "sepsis" is defined as a state of putrefaction or decay, and it is often fatal. The patient's organs systemically shut down and once it sets in, the road back is almost impossible.

"Mark," the doctor said with the bedside manner of a steam engine, "your wife may not live through the night."

The doctors were forced to induce a comalike state as

Hannah's organs began failing. The family began to pray, begging God for a miracle, and they even had a faith healer visit.

Several days after Hannah was admitted, I visited the hospital. After seeing Hannah and praying over her unresponsive body, I gathered the family to ask God for healing. I begged God to spare my friend's life, and pleaded with Him to work a miracle. As I prayed, the wailing in the room was so intense, I had to almost shout.

In the evenings, Mark sang in Hannah's ear. He delivered all three verses of "Great Is Thy Faithfulness," and he sometimes selected a random tune from a hymnal he had. On one occasion, just after midnight, Mark pulled out his phone and played Glover's "It's You (I Have Loved)" and sang along. When the tune concluded, he leaned down and whispered in Hannah's ear one of the catchphrases from their marriage: "You know I'm crazy about you, don't you?"

Days turned into weeks, June became July, and the situation grew more dire by the day. Hannah's blood wasn't circulating to her extremities, and since she wasn't conscious, Mark had to make the decision to allow the doctors to amputate both arms and both legs.

On August 4, Hannah woke briefly and Mark explained the details of the surgery they'd performed while she was sleeping. Though Hannah wasn't fully cognizant, she understood what he'd said. She began to cry. Shaking from emotion, Mark said he was sorry. Hannah mouthed *I love you* and made a kissing face before drifting off again.

For another month, Hannah languished in the intensive care unit. The doctor broke the news to Mark that Hannah would never recover. Though everyone was astounded by her will to live, it only delayed the inevitable. Mark knew that at some deep subconscious level, Hannah was holding on for his sake.

He entered her room late that night when no one was around and leaned in close. Pushing through sobs, Mark told her that he loved her with every fiber of his being, but if she needed to leave, he would be okay. For a moment, the rate on Hannah's heart monitor jumped, and he took that as a sign that she'd heard him.

On September 5, all of Hannah's vital organs were failing, and she wasn't able to breathe on her own. The family gathered around and sang "Amazing Grace" over her. For the last verse, they simply repeated the word "Hallelujah." And then, at 4:17 a.m., Hannah Rinehart passed from this life into the next. She left behind a husband, both parents, and many friends who loved her deeply.

When I received news of Hannah's death, I sat down on my couch and wept. I was angry with God—that He didn't bring healing, that He let it drag on for so long, that He couldn't find it in Himself to work a miracle. *Why, God? Why now, why her, and why this way? What kind of God would sit on His hands and allow such a thing to happen to one of His own? Not a very good one.*

* * *

My frustration with God exposed that at some level I still clung to the false belief that following Jesus is a process of investment and reward. As I sink into Christ, I instinctively sit back to rake in the blessings. Financial flourishing. Rescue. Protection. When I notice a fellow sheep suffering, I think, *Oh my. How can this be? They've followed Jesus so closely.* If sheep follow the Shepherd, shouldn't they be protected from the wolves of ruin, depression, poverty, divorce?

One of Teresa of Avila's evening prayers included the observation: "So this is how You treat Your friends; no wonder You have so few." Whenever I read that line, I wonder if she had Abraham, famed for being a "friend of God," in mind.[1] Rather than live a life of pleasure, free of pain, Abraham's journey was marked by frustration and suffering and a series of difficult demands made of him by God. Though Abraham was faithful all his life, he died a homeless wanderer, buried in a foreign land.

Why would God allow such hardship to befall those who trust in Him? People like Abraham and Hannah and all the rest of us whom God counts as "friends"?[2] Or anyone, for that matter?

In the months following Hannah's death, I kept asking, "Why does God allow suffering?" I wrestled with the question in my heart and mind. Even commentaries and theological treatises provided little comfort. Somewhere along the way, I began asking a different question: "Where is God in the suffering?" This was a question God seemed more ready to answer.

The first question does not seem to have an answer, and even if it did, it would not alleviate my grief. The pain of suffering will always exceed the logic of our explanations. And the benefit of the second answer is what provides more than information. It provides illumination, inspiration, and encouragement. If I truly want to pursue God in a world where depravity often reigns, I need to shift my eyes from the logic of suffering and become fixated on the location of a Savior in the midst of it all.

One of the Scripture's favorite metaphors for Jesus is the Good Shepherd. He is a benevolent sheepherder, the image asserts, and we are His faithful flock of braying sheep. Often when I've heard people teach on this imagery, they tend to focus on sheep's lack of intelligence. They portray sheep as dumb animals who are unable to care for themselves and need a shepherd so they don't die from dumbness. Their sole purposes are for shearing and slaughtering. It's not a very flattering picture for a church to hear, particularly for those in attendance who aren't Christians. The implicit message of this metaphor is "You need Jesus because you're stupid."

Modern science is revealing that sheep aren't as unintelligent as portrayed in church circles. Sheep can be taught to perform many of the same tricks as dogs, and while they're not the most brilliant creatures, they're a far cry from the least intelligent. The larger problem with teaching that sheep are dumb is that if we believe this, then when we read the nearly seven hundred references to sheep in the Bible we'll interpret them as God saying, *You are dumb, you are dumb, you are dumb*, when nothing could be further from the truth.

God did not create sheep to be dumb, but He did create them defenseless. Unlike other animals, they don't have sharp teeth or claws. They don't have straight pointy horns. Even the sound they make—*baaah*—isn't scary. The only defense mechanism God gave sheep is to stay within a flock under the watchful eye of a shepherd. Understanding sheep in this way makes the Scriptures spring to life.

One of the most extensive uses of shepherd imagery is found in John 10. Here, Jesus says that when the shepherd enters the gate, the sheep follow because they know His voice. When He calls them, their ears perk and their feet begin to shuffle. They know better than to follow a stranger, and if one tries to trick them, the sheep will scatter.

"When He has brought out all His own," John writes, "He goes on ahead of them, and His sheep follow Him because they know His voice."[3]

When we read this passage with fresh eyes, it seems like Jesus is actually giving sheep the credit they are due. More than fluffy pets or farm animals, sheep are designed to respond to the voice of their shepherd.

The idea that sheep are dumb pack animals is a myth[4] that was begun by cowboys. It spread particularly far in America during the U.S. range wars between sheep and cattle farmers in the nineteenth century. The reason many cowboys held this view is because sheep and cattle behave quite differently. Cows are herded from the rear with snapping whips and electric prods, while sheep prefer a gentler guide who stands out front. Cattle are *driven*; sheep must be *led*.

Rather than demeaning His listeners, Jesus is displaying His understanding of our deepest human tendencies. Much of His audience knew that sheep prefer to go only where a shepherd has gone first. By waiting on their shepherd to scope things out, sheep are making sure they're entering trusted territory.

What difference does this make? Quite a lot, as it turns out, because the Good Shepherd ended up languishing from a cross. He too knows what pain, rejection, injustice, loneliness, betrayal, and, yes, thinking God is giving you the cold shoulder feels like.

Jesus did not live like I'd expect a God-man should. He became a God who suffered—an unheard of concept to the ancients and one that is foreign to modern readers still. Buddha died peacefully at eighty years old, surrounded by his friends and disciples. Confucius also died an elderly man, and he'd gained prominence as a Chinese sage. Muhammad died in the arms of one of his wives having become a powerful ruler of many in Arabia.[5] But Jesus's life was snuffed out at a young age when He was executed by the most brutal means.

My relationship with Jesus carries with it the promise that He will never ask me to go where He does not lead, and He fits in a long line of Christian pupils, prophets, and preachers who discovered that with God no one has to suffer alone.

It's the promise of Moses that when I stand on the mountaintop and look over a promised land I'll never enter, God will be there to take me home.

It's the promise of Samson that even when I mess up, God doesn't quit on me.

It's the promise of David that when the enemies come knocking, I'll have a God to hear my prayers.

It's the promise of Shadrach, Meshach, and Abednego that when the king sends me to the furnace, He'll stand in the fire with me.

It's the promise of Daniel that I'll never face the lions alone.

It's the promise of Ruth that when life seems hopeless, the Redeemer is still working on my behalf.

It's the promise of Stephen that even in death God will watch over me.

It's the promise of Paul that when I sit alone in life's prison, I'm never alone. God will give me a song.

It's the promise of John that when I feel isolated in the caves of life, exiled to the most distant island, I am not without vision.

And it's the promise of Jesus that I can trust Him when He asks me to pick up my cross because when I follow Him to Golgotha, He'll hang there next to me.

I'm a lot like Thomas, famed for his doubting. In the Gospels, Christ finally appears to Thomas with nail holes in His wrists. This story has always perplexed me. *If Christ shows up in a fully healed body, one in which He ascended back into heaven, why wasn't His body perfected? Why did Jesus still bear the scars from the Roman barbarians?*

Then I realize that unlike the song I sang in church as a child, Jesus is not "the all-time, undisputed, undefeated champion." Instead, He is the Broken One, the Suffering Servant, the One who meets us with a visibly scarred body. And the longer I live, the more I find myself limping behind Him.

As Barbara Brown Taylor says, "The way you recognize the Christ—and His followers—is not by their muscles, but by their scars."[6]

God does not rush around the china shop of life making sure the teacups don't fall off a ledge and break. Rather He stays ever present as the gracious shopkeeper, picking up the cracked porcelain, supergluing it, and placing it among His most prized possessions.

When I understand what Jesus means when He calls Himself the Good Shepherd, I see myself differently. Rather than a fool without enough sense not to fly kites in a thunderstorm, Jesus knows I am a cautious creature who needs a leader who blazes the trail before me and waits for me there.

* * *

Six months after Hannah's passing, I sat across a table from Mark. We poked at our eggs until I broke the silence to ask how he'd been holding up. He told me he was still grieving.

He had been having a recurring dream where Hannah was back and life had returned to normal. They'd spend what seemed like hours in each other's company doing all their favorite things. Over the course of the dream, he'd get used to living with her again. But when they'd finally go to bed and he'd turn off the light, Mark would wake suddenly and have to begin the grieving process again.

"Don't you ever wonder where God is in all of this?" I asked.

"Actually, this has made my faith stronger," Mark replied. "I don't understand God, and I don't understand why He allowed this. I miss Hannah, but I've never felt alone."

Astounded, I asked for details. Mark said that he's felt God walking alongside him the whole time. When he didn't know what to do, he'd pray for people to come and someone would always show up. People he hadn't seen in years would e-mail or call him and give him exactly what he needed. When Mark was facing overwhelming expenses as a result of the situation, a not-for-profit stepped in to help raise money to offset the costs. Through it all, he's witnessed how tragedy can forge unlikely friendships and even bring God glory.

"Death is natural," Mark says. "Hannah's just came in an unexpected way. But as I consider how God has been with me, I'm able to start remembering Hannah not with tears, but a smile."

In an unlikely way, Mark has seen the Good Shepherd at work. Through it, he has learned what all God's followers must: that chasing after Jesus in this perilous world often means being led to places he'd rather not go. But it also means that he won't have to go there alone.

• • •

I've always suffered from acrophobia, which is a fancy way of saying I'm afraid of heights. I trembled when I visited the Empire State Building, standing with my back against the inner wall and inching my way around the perimeter, and I sometimes get weak-kneed climbing a ladder to change a lightbulb. Nothing can make me hyperventilate more quickly than being in a high, open space.

I remember visiting Madrid, Spain, with some old friends. On our first day, we walked down to the Almudena Cathedral. Construction on this neo-Gothic monolith began in 1879 and continued for a century. When you first witness the scale of this monstrosity, you can understand why. My friends and I climbed the unending stairs to the pinnacle where we found a perch overlooking the city. The others wanted to take a picture on that spot to commemorate our visit, but I balked. One by one, they all stepped atop the lookout and waved for me to come.

If they can do it, I can do it, I reasoned.

With one step and then two, I made my way to where they were and carefully turned for our Kodak moment. After it was over, my adrenaline was pumping. I slipped down and caught my breath, realizing I would have missed the experience had they not gone before me.

"Sure," you say, "but unlike Hannah, you returned from the lookout. The difference in your story is that you came back from the ledge, but she didn't get to come back to life."

That, of course, depends on where you believe each story ends.

If you ask me, Hannah's story did not end in the hospital room or casket. Her saga continues. Mark's lullaby was not the last she'll hear. When Jesus languishes on His cross, He teaches us that tragedy never has the final word. "Life is bloody and unfair, but fear not, wooly wanderers," Jesus says. "Resurrection will come."

When I decide to follow the Good Shepherd, I am able to step into the unknown and uncertain places with confidence because

Jesus has already been there. I can take up my cross because He has already hung from His own. So when tragedy beckons, I hear His voice, and I follow Him, and He promises me eternal life, and I will never perish, and nothing can snatch me from His hand. Not suffering or difficulty or physical death. For the Good Shepherd stands beside me, leading me through that shadowy valley on my way to still waters.

8

Revelation at the Ping-Pong Emporium

Encountering Jesus in Sacrilege

There is nothing so secular that it cannot be sacred, and that is one of the deepest messages of the Incarnation.
—MADELEINE L'ENGLE

Three decades ago, Grant Henry was a God-fearing churchgoer who wanted nothing more than to please the Almighty. His parents took him to a local congregation three times a week, where he'd fill his spiritual tank with Sunday school lessons, twenty-minute sermons, and a handful of hymns. So zealous was his religious fervor that he pursued a master's in pastoral care from Princeton Theological Seminary.

After working in churchland for several years, his passion waned and his faith faded. He soon found himself standing in a chasm between the American church and the sort of faith he believed Jesus promoted. Rather than work at reforming the institution, he left Christianity altogether.

Grant Henry shepherds a different kind of congregation today. He's the owner of Sister Louisa's Church of the Living Room and Ping-Pong Emporium (nicknamed CHURCH). Nestled in Atlanta's Old Fourth Ward, a gentrifying district in the heart of the city, this bar has become a hipster hangout, a gathering place for the dechurched, and a regular happy hour stop for the obscenely beautiful casts of *Drop Dead Diva* and *Vampire Diaries*. The Web site says the doors open for worship daily at five p.m., but you'd better come early if you want to snag a barstool and partake of cheap beer and Hebrew National chili dogs.

More than anything, Sister Louisa's is a place to hang out, a social club of sorts. As *Atlanta* magazine observed, Sister

Louisa's "is more about fellowship than sacrilege."[1] The bar is full of broken people, many of whom seem to pretend to have everything together. Patrons cock their heads back to belly laugh, keeping conversation light and others at arm's length.

My first visit to CHURCH plunged me into a sea of conflicting emotions—curiosity, amusement, annoyance, and displeasure by turns. A bouncer greeted me at the front door from behind a scarred pulpit positioned next to a sign that said COME ON IN, PRECIOUS. Once I was inside, a hodgepodge of tacky religious décor assaulted me. A statuette of the Virgin Mary stood conspicuously behind the liquor bottles. Choir robes hung on the coatrack to my left.

"Welcome to CHURCH, brother," the bartender shouted. "Can I get you some spiritual sangria?"

I stepped up to the bar and ordered a hot dog with all the fixins called the "Church Picnic," because, as the menu boasts, "Jesus loves our coleslaw." Rather than wait for my food to arrive, I toured the two-story facility. Artwork covered almost every square inch of the exposed brick walls. A vintage 1700s Yugoslavian confessional rested in the corner. Grant planned to transform the confessional into a photo booth, the bartender later informed me, but feared too many people would "relive their childhood abuse experiences." Upstairs, crosses fashioned from neon lights hung on the walls. A Ping-Pong table stood proudly in the center, encircled by oak pews where patrons can cheer on players. No televisions hang in Sister Louisa's, but I was promised that church organ karaoke would soon begin.

How can such a place thrive in a Bible Belt town like Atlanta? Why doesn't the community protest this sacrilegious establishment and put it out of business?

My hot dog arrived, and I pushed through the anger-induced nausea to choke it down.

· · ·

The word "sacrilege" originates from the Latin *sacer* ("sacred") and *legere* ("to steal"). In Roman times, it referred to the plundering of temples and graves. Sacrilege is an attack on religious places, people, and ideas. But what I've noticed is that often the people and places labeled "sacrilegious" aren't stealing the sacred after all; they are mocking the thin shell of pseudo-righteousness often painted over those things. They are pointing to the holy emperor and telling the crowds the truth about his nakedness.

Those in Sister Louisa's seem to understand what many modern Christians have forgotten: what we call religion is often a malformation of true faith, one that's calcified and crystallized and hardened. Rather than a vibrant adventure of knowing and loving God, it is a rigid, formalized, power-seeking, oppressive way of trying to be good or look good or feel good.[2]

Sister Louisa's is an irreverent place that pokes fun at faith like it's a competition, but more than that, it's a commentary on American Christianity by someone who once waded in it chest-deep. In some ways, the critique is quite accurate.

A vintage rendering of a woman with an updo chides, "The higher the hair, the closer to God," exposing the pretentiousness of modern-day churchgoers. Riffing on the feel-good, self-helpy gospel preached in many congregations, one art piece declares, "It is our duty to catapult each other into greatness." As a knock on the corporate elements of the institutional church, a baby doll climbs a cross with the phrase LADDER OF SUCCESS scribbled across the horizontal beam. Block letters nailed next to the bar spell out OH R U GOD as a face-slapping annotation about Christians' judgmentalism. A wooden placard depicting "a good Christian boy" hangs in the bathroom. Numbered rules outline the laws that one must follow to get in good with God. The difference between *this* church, however, and many real ones is that no one here pretends to obey them.

I couldn't help noticing the analysis of Christian partisanship. A yard sign near the front entrance says CHRIST FOR STATE SENATE, while another art piece simply states JESUS LOVES DICK CHENEY. An illustration of Jesus sitting on the side of a mountain exclaims, "I can see Russia from my rock!"

These pieces remind me that "religion" attempts to build a box in which God lives. It ties down the Almighty with the constraints of routines and rules and limitations and political affiliations. Religion says that God does only certain things in certain ways, no more and no less. That God is who we *think* God is, and nothing else. But faith knows better. Faith knows that God's calling card is surprise and that what many label as Christianity is just baggage we're forcing true faith to lug.

The word "religion" is used negatively almost every time it appears in the Bible with one glaring exception: "Pure and genuine religion in the sight of God the Father means caring for orphans and widows in their distress and refusing to let the world corrupt you."[3]

The kind of spirituality that God desires—this unfettered faith—speaks kindly, promotes justice, cares for the marginalized and the have-nots, and strives to be loving, joyful, peaceful, patient, and gentle even when the world pulls in the opposite direction.

What the apostle James calls "pure religion" turns out not to be religion at all. This unfettered faith is a new element on the periodic table of life. It is made up of unknown molecules, and one has to mine deeply to excavate it. When it has been chiseled out and dusted off, at least two differences emerge.

First, unfettered faith places a premium on love. In Isaiah 58, God's people are incensed. They rush around trying to do as much for God as possible, and yet He seems so far away. "Why do we fast but You do not see? Why humble ourselves when You do not notice?"

When God answers, His words shock the askers: "It is not I who have forsaken you, but you have forsaken Me. If you cannot hear Me, it is because you have strayed far from My voice. It is not I who am ignoring you, but you who are ignoring Me."[4]

Sometimes I act just like the Israelites. I rush around trying to squeeze God into my life whenever I have a spare moment. I make it to church on Sundays—because I know I should—and say a quick prayer before meals. I try to avoid "bad" activities and "bad" people and "bad" places as much as possible. But when I call to God in the hushed moments, I hear only the sound of my voice.

Being in a relationship with God is a tough place to be. When I've heard others say that following Jesus has made life easy for them, I can't help thinking how different my experience has been. Sure, I've experienced countless blessings and benefits in my spiritual journey. But it has also been a struggle.

A life committed to God requires me to do things I don't always want to do. I feel the nudge to help others, and I groan at the inconvenience. When I'm rude or selfish or unkind, I wrestle with the aftermath. When I know I should share the good news of Jesus with someone, I let my fear and insecurity get the best of me. The process of refinement is painful, and this road called faith has never been a cakewalk for me.

When my spiritual pursuits grow difficult, I have a tendency to try to shake God off my back or convince Him to scram and give me some space. I usually attempt to do this by either breaking or keeping all the "rules."

The Israelites in the story took the latter approach. They had been obeying God's every command—fasting and praying and cleansing themselves. When it was time to make atonement, they trekked to the temple and slayed lambs and doves. But when they listened for God's voice, all they heard was the sound of tumbleweeds. In their religious pursuits, they failed to love their neighbors and missed God.[5]

No wonder Jesus found himself at bitter odds with the most "righteous" and "religious" people while He was on earth. He frequently disregarded the law and the religious establishment with such boldness that reading the Gospels often offends our Pharisee hearts as much as it did our religious ancestors two millennia ago. In the short time He was on earth, Jesus ate with every kind of terrible person you could imagine. He touched a leper and a corpse. And He failed to honor the Sabbath—one of the Ten Commandments—without a second's struggle. Jesus was a rule breaker and so were His disciples. Worse still, Jesus talked about a narrow gate into God's kingdom and told the rule followers they may not make it through.

Why?

He was making the statement that what ultimately counts is not how many rules I follow or winning every theological debate or being well regarded by influencers and power brokers. What matters is how I love God and others. These are the two greatest commandments of all time. Put these first, and I'll demonstrate I understand the rest.

Unfettered faith also replaces the self with the Savior. One of Jesus's most memorable stories was about two brothers and a father. One day, the younger brother gets a wild hair and tells his dad he'd like to take his share of the family inheritance early. After the older brother presumably tries to talk him out of it, the father relents and hands over the dough. The son is gone before his dad can say good-bye, and soon the son has squandered every penny.

After being driven to utter poverty in a foreign town, the humbled son decides to return home and ask his father to let him become a servant on the family farm. At least he'll have food to eat. But the homecoming turns out much different than he expected. When his dad sees his silhouette resolve on the horizon, he runs to meet him and invites everyone to come to a welcome-home party.

But something fascinating happens at the end of the story that I missed for most of my life. Jesus closes this narrative with a note about the elder son, who remained silent until now. "I can't believe you're throwing that ungrateful punk a party," the older son protests. "I've been working for you faithfully for years, and my inheritance is still in the bank. You've never thrown a party for me."[6]

At first, Jesus's reference to the elder son seems like a meaningless addendum. But when I consider the rest of His ministry—from avoiding the religious leaders' schemes and trick questions to excoriating the Pharisees for their self-righteousness—I begin to see Jesus setting up a contrast between true faith and the spirit of religion. The younger son returns to his dad—humbled and disgraced, asking for nothing except the father's embrace—while the elder son is so consumed with anger that he can't count to ten.

What we often call religion pursues God for the wrong reasons (out of guilt and fear rather than joy), and it is driven by the wrong compulsions (to be right above all rather than to be loving at any expense). But perhaps most devastating, it is focused on the wrong person (the worshiper rather than the worshiped). When I follow religion, I look inward and outward, rather than upward.[7]

Another commentary on this is found in Mark 11 when Jesus curses a fig tree, a peculiar act for modern readers. Ancient audiences, however, would have known that the tree was a symbol of the religious system in Israel. So when Jesus curses the tree, He is making a scandalous statement about the religious establishment. "It's fruitless. It's worthless," Jesus is saying. "It has grown up among us, and we've gotten entangled in its branches, but now look—it's withered and dead and not worth anything."[8] When Jesus curses this tree, He is judging it, removing it, and replacing it with something else—Himself.[9]

• • •

Sister Louisa's was about the most unexpected place to find Jesus that I could have imagined, but I believe that God inhabits every cubic inch of this spinning ball of dirt we call earth, so I knew He must be somewhere.

"What did you make of all the images in this place when you first encountered them?" I asked the bartender.

"Like most people, I initially mistook all this for simple sacrilege," he replied. "But now I get it. Grant's artwork forces people to examine their beliefs by using shock to expose the hypocrisy and judgmentalism that he experienced when he was a part of the Christian religion."

My judgment turned to empathy as I considered the earliest memories of my spiritual journey.

I'd felt overwhelmed by the rules and the restrictions, the need to be righteous. I'd staved off guilt with confession and tried my best to hide any doubts that plagued me in the quiet moments. Despite the heavy burdens, I'd executed my religion with near perfection for years. But I'd wandered through life estranged from true faith.

The religion I practiced was quick to condemn, slow to offer grace, and weighed down by need to be evermore holy. In my Ahab-like pursuit of piety, I paid little attention to those in need. Life seemed a never-ending roller coaster that rushed from the hill of pride in my good behavior to the valley of remorse for even the slightest wrongdoing. I found myself in church as much as any other space as I lunged forward to embrace God. My voice belted out hymns in youth choir. I volunteered for various ministries and memorized Scriptures by the fistful. Yet despite my best efforts, I nurtured a creeping intuition that the God I'd been envisioning and the Jesus of the Bible were worlds apart.

Part of me always wanted to run from Christianity. As a pastor's child, I'd seen the nasty entrails of the Christian church. And unlike some, my pursuit of Jesus hasn't been a parking lot. It's been more like an obstacle course sprinkled with interesting people who've served as conduits of God's grace. But still I strain, reaching out with arms fully extended.

Along the way, I've bumped into others who have had similar experiences. Chloe was raised in a strict Christian home. She obeyed all the Christian rules—no drinking, no smoking, no swearing, and, of course, no naughty sex with her boyfriend. Once out of her parents' home, she tried checking off the list of dos and don'ts during early adulthood. She decided to walk away once she realized religion couldn't bring her joy or peace, fulfillment or contentment.

Michael was a classmate from high school who seemed adroit in Christian apologetics. If a skeptical student attacked Christianity, he was the first to turn them back with carefully rehearsed arguments. When I ran into him in a grocery store checkout line years later, he told me he doesn't ascribe to any religious tradition. His college religion professor spun his spiritual logic around with counterarguments. Because he saw Christianity as a series of rational arguments, the religion of his adolescence slipped like sand between his fingers.

And then there's Michelle, who began attending church after she had children. Michelle longed for her children to acquire a strong ethical framework, and the local Christian congregation seemed the most commonsense place for such things. Three years later, she watched the church build expensive buildings while much of the community around it crumbled in poverty. *I thought Christianity was supposed to make you a good person,* she thought as she left the church for the final time.

Standing in CHURCH, the images and words that had offended me moments earlier were now pushing me to reflect on those areas in my life where I'd chosen the practice of a dead religion over a love affair with a living God, where I, like Michael and Michelle and Chloe, have built my faith on sand. My shoulders came down from around my ears and settled atop my back once more. My breathing slowed to a relaxed pace, and clenched fists became open hands.

. . .

When Jesus selected his friends and those who would inhabit his inner circle, He looked outside of the religious aristocracy. He picked outsiders and rebels, zealots and tax collectors, sinners and scandalous women. Jesus loved everyone, I am sure, but He didn't seem to *like* the Pharisees.

Jesus "made the most morally disciplined group of the day, Pharisees, the object of His criticism. In fact, Jesus seems to have been in perpetual conflict with the 'good people' of His day and ironically justified His consorting with 'bad people' by the remark that not those who are healthy, but those who are sick, are in need of a physician."[10]

Millions of Jews inhabited the earth when Jesus was alive, but scholars say only about six thousand of them were Pharisees. Yet Jesus disproportionately hones in on this small group throughout His ministry. Perhaps because He knew the Pharisees' ranks would swell over the next two thousand years.

The Pharisees, like many of their modern descendants, sequestered themselves from nonbelievers, lawbreakers, and the lower classes. The priests even possessed a private bridge linking their homes to the temple so they wouldn't have to mingle with the common people. But Jesus's ministry shatters this paradigm, and rankles the religious elites in the process.

We see this on grand display when Jesus visits John to be baptized. As a teenager, I learned that this passage was about God's desire for me to get dunked in a swimming pool at youth camp. And while it may likely demonstrate Jesus's example in baptism, I think there's more here that should not be missed.

As the scruffy, rough-edged John waits in the waist-deep water, a line forms in front of him. His message of "repent and be baptized" has undoubtedly connected with this crowd, and sinners have gathered to be cleansed by the wilderness prophet. In the distance, Jesus approaches, and one can't help but wonder what He plans to do. Will He poke the sinful masses in the chest and condemn them for their wickedness? Will He stand on the riverbanks and clap from a distance as they come out of the water, praising their intentions to live a better life?

Nope.

Jesus gets in line with them.

This was outrageous and risky for someone about to begin a very public ministry. By stepping in line, Jesus was loading ammunition into every Jewish gossiper's gun. *Why would that rabbi be getting in line with the bad guys? What has He done that He needs to repent of or ask forgiveness for?* But Jesus isn't deterred by the rumors that may follow or the headlines His actions might create. He steps up to wait His turn.

Even the New Testament writers struggle with the scandal of what Jesus has done. Mark tells the story but moves on quickly. Matthew elaborates on Mark's account, but he makes sure to add that John tried to talk Jesus out of it. Luke avoids mentioning that the controversial wilderness preacher was the one who performed the baptism. And John is more anxious than any of the others, and he skips over the baptism completely and only tells of seeing the Spirit descend like a dove on Christ. Scholars say that all this uneasiness is evidence that John really did baptize Jesus that day alongside all those repentant sinners, because when someone tells you something when it is not in his best interest, he is probably telling you the truth.[11]

This bold move by Christ set the tone for the radical ministry that followed. Jesus did not just *call* sinners; He identified with them, befriended them, dwelled among them. At the river that day, Jesus tips us off to whose side He's on, and it's not the side most would have predicted or even advised.

Over the years, as my personal flaws have become more broadly known, I've noticed a growing distance separating me from some of my closest friends. I resist the temptation to judge their hearts knowing I have often acted in similar ways. I too have avoided people either because I'm being a snob or because I think they're "sinful." Avoiding them makes me feel a bit more holy. These are people who upset us because we think they upset God.[12]

Sometimes they have names or are just *types* of people I try to avoid. I convince myself that by dodging them or pushing them away, I keep their dirtiness off my righteous self, never recognizing that if I think that way, perhaps the reverse is true. Jesus took the opposite approach, seeking out those who most religious people would have stiff-armed. Maybe that's one reason Jesus often had disdain for the religious establishment—because He spent so much time with people who'd been hurt by it.

But not only did Jesus hang out with "unholy" people, He hung out in "unholy" places. The dinner tables of tax collectors, parties thrown by immoral socialites, and, perhaps most reprehensible, wells in Samaria. This in contrast to the God of many modern Christians who is sterile and sequestered, never disrupted in His holy habitation. But Jesus enters the places most people didn't think was fit for God, much less a rabbi from Nazareth. Luckily, Jesus never set out to be homecoming king. He had other plans.

*   *   *

Avoid even the appearance of evil," the youth group volunteer chided me, her bony finger wagging in my eleven-year-old face. I'd been standing in a hallway with some friends having a harmless conversation about schoolwork, but it didn't matter. It *appeared* that we *might* be up to no good, and that was sinful enough.

The verse she referenced is popular among conservative Christians, but there's just one not-so-tiny problem: It doesn't exist. At least not technically. It appears in 1 Thessalonians 5:22 in the King James Version of the Bible but is absent in all modern translations. As a child, I never questioned why the phrasing could only be found in one five-hundred-year-old rendering or why the Epistles would command something so utterly irreconcilable with the life and ministry of Jesus. My elders believed it, so I too accepted it as gospel truth.

Who was I to argue with God's word?

In my earliest years, I believed that if a restaurant's dining room was full, I couldn't sit at the bar lest someone think I was palling around with riffraff. I wasn't to be seen outside a theater hanging with "the wrong crowd" because, well, there was some saying about birds of a feather that prohibited it. Earrings on a man meant he had questionable sexuality, a bottle of wine on the dinner table meant you might be an alcoholic, and a boy and a girl in a room alone together meant they probably just got freaky.

This was the most oppressive verse I could imagine, promoting a cloistered life that was hermetically sealed off from any people or places or activities that any onlooker might raise a brow over. It created ironclad boundaries where nearly everything except going to church was morally suspect. So I drove myself mad by perpetually self-evaluating what other people might be thinking of me.

Scholars now agree that the proper translation of 1 Thessalonians 5:22 verse is something like, "Avoid every kind of evil." Or more directly from the Greek, "No matter what form evil takes, abstain from it." Rather than yoking Christians, this passage liberates them to "hold fast to that which is good."

Many well-meaning pastors and parents favored this one mistranslation as they sought to protect their children and/or congregants. Others simply cherry-picked. Mistranslation leads to misapplication, but too few Christians do their homework when it comes to the Bible. Instead, they exhibit a dangerous tendency among many Christians and churches today: ignoring any translations or interpretations except those that support one's predetermined viewpoint.

Jesus demonstrated what a Godward life looks like by avoiding sin but never avoiding sinful people or "unholy places." The Pharisees couldn't comprehend such a posture because they served a God who dwelled on the mountaintop and confined Himself to the holy of holies. He couldn't even *look* on dirty people and places. But we forfeit our illusions of social separateness when we meet Emmanuel—"God *with* us." Jesus is the one who seeks out people we may find repugnant or unclean or unfit for friendship. Jesus signals an in-breaking of divine presence, a removal of barriers we place between sacred and secular or even sinful.[13]

Jesus is better than I imagined because He shatters my strivings for sterility with a radical invitation to live free. Free *from* sinful patterns, but also free from moralism, free from legalism, and free from condemnation. Free *to* love the unlovable, to use your gifts to serve those in need, to share the great story of redemption through Christ with others. Jesus liberates me from the ball and chain of religion and releases me from a cold life of moralistic perfectionism. This kind of God is almost too incredible to accept, and yet there He stands nonetheless.

*   *   *

When I returned home after my first visit to CHURCH, I had to take a shower to wash the smell of cigarettes off my body.

As the water gushed out of the faucet, I saw an image for my spiritual tendencies. Following Jesus is like bathing in the living water, and if I am not careful, calcium deposits can build up over time. Rejuvenating spiritual disciplines can become the mildew of empty ritual. Concern for my spiritual journey can become the fungus of self-centered faith. The slimy film of religion can accumulate without my noticing it.

Eugene Peterson describes this tendency this way:

> Imagine yourself moving into a house with a huge picture window overlooking a grand view across a wide expanse of water enclosed by a range of snowcapped mountains... Several times a day you interrupt your work and stand before this window to take in the majesty and the beauty... One afternoon you notice some bird droppings on the window glass, get a bucket of water and a towel, and clean it... Another day visitors come with a tribe of small dirty-fingered children. The moment they leave you see all the smudge marks on the glass. They are hardly out the door before you have the bucket out... Keeping that window clean develops into an obsessive-compulsive neurosis. You accumulate ladders and buckets and squeegees. You construct a scaffolding both inside and out to make it possible to get to all the difficult corners and heights. You have the cleanest window in North America—but it's now been years since you looked through it. You've become a Pharisee.[14]

Places like CHURCH expose the dangerous habits in my own life. They reveal where I've neurotically worked my religious fingers to the bone and robbed myself of the joy of knowing Jesus in the process.

As I reconsidered all I'd seen that night, I could feel the disgruntled ex-minister's frustration and heartache. The disdain for the Christian religious establishment was unmistakable, but the cry for a real encounter with God was deafening—ringing in every brushstroke and religious icon. In this way, the irreverent sacrilege draped on the walls sounded more like echoes of my heart's cry for Jesus, pure and simple.

My heart had grown thin from a rules-based "do more" religion. I yearned to trade a system of divine formulas more concerned with constructing arguments than opening my arms to a God who transcends human logic. CHURCH pushed me from striving for God's acceptance to relishing the living God.

If Jesus lived in Atlanta, I think He'd probably be friends with Grant Henry. If He were hankering for a hot dog while driving through the Old Fourth Ward, He might even stop by CHURCH. In fact, I think Jesus would have felt right at home in that corner bar because, like Grant, Jesus would have been saddened by the hypocrisy and judgmentalism and oppressive religiosity of those who bear Christ's name. The only difference is that Jesus would offer a better path to God: Himself.

At my core, I crave wholeness. I'm like the line of people waiting for John's baptism so long ago. I know I need something, even though I don't always recognize that what I'm looking for is standing right beside me. The hunger for wholeness is often felt greatest in places like Sister Louisa's, where people have given up all pretense of being perfect.

While I don't seek out or create sacrilege, I realize that encountering it is unavoidable. In films and music and paintings and relationships. In a snarky article online, a cutting joke on a television show, or a passing comment from a neighbor or friend, I encounter reactions and affronts to God and Jesus and all the malformations of both.

Often, I dismiss it as the anger of a faith hater, but a nugget of truth is usually buried somewhere in the criticism. This can be an opportunity for sanctification if I refuse to react, get offended, or turn and run. Rather than be repulsed, maybe I should reflect. *What does this expose in my heart? Where have I missed the mark?*

Ever since my first visit to CHURCH, I've been learning to pause and consider what God might be up to in sacrilegious spaces. Rather than focusing on how much those who offend me need to repent of their sin, I'm discovering occasions to repent of my self-righteousness.

Now when I encounter sacrilege, I don't bolt for the door. I run toward what God wants to reveal in the stubborn chambers of my heart.

9

A Tableless Home

Encountering Jesus in Absence

God is the God who appears from behind the God who has disappeared.

—PAUL TILLICH

Walking the streets of Kathmandu is like guest starring in an Indiana Jones movie. Once thought to be the fabled Shangri-La, the capital city of Nepal has remained largely unchanged since the Middle Ages. Monks in colorful clothes mix with bearded adventurers who've just finished climbing Mount Everest. Steep staircases lead to hidden temples. Taxicabs and rickshaws race through the narrow streets, and the smell of fresh-made momo dumplings and dried chili peppers summon hungry tourists.

I had visited Kathmandu to work in a group home for abandoned or orphaned children, where I played with them, helped them with their homework, and came to love them. If the children finished their studies in time, we'd climb on top of the roof and play. Sometimes I'd pause to stare at the city, houses stumbling on top of each other divided by a rancid river slicing through like a dirty bread knife. On a clear day, I could see Everest in the distance, but most days it hid behind a dreary blanket of smog.

At night, we'd gather around the outside wall of an empty dining room while our meal was assembled in the center. They didn't even have a table. Prior to eating, we'd sing Christian worship songs in Nepali and English. While the food cooled, we'd sometimes sing for hours. Clapping. Dancing. Shouting praise while one of the children played a guitar lacking a couple of strings.

Here I learned a lesson about communal worship. In America, we often criticize church services where everything does not suit our liking. Maybe the music was too loud. Or too quiet. Or perhaps the words on the high-definition screens didn't transition fast enough for us to keep up. In Nepal, we didn't have any of the technological flourishes I was accustomed to, and the absence of such things set us free to worship in pure form.

Some time after dinner the night before I left, I said my good-byes and walked back to my hotel room in the pitch-blackness. The city's rationed electricity had long been clamped and few families were fortunate enough to have generators. Along my stroll, I'd peer into candlelit rooms where butchers chopped the next day's meat and families gathered for conversation. My mind wandered back to those children, and my heart filled with pity. I imagine there's a special pain felt by those who've lost their birth parents.

One might assume that returning home would be a welcomed event, but it wasn't, for the experience had left me feeling deeply disappointed by God. *How could You abandon these children who love You so much? They haven't done anything to deserve this.*

    •   •   •

Most people of faith can remember the first time they felt that God let them down. Maybe they begged God to heal their mother's illness, but God didn't grant it. Or perhaps they prayed each night on bended knee for the restoration of their marriage, only to walk through the emotional gauntlet of divorce. Or maybe they felt a calling on their lives to pursue a particular vocation. It was an inclination they just couldn't shake. Each night, they asked God to open a door to a job where they could use their gifts and talents, but more than a decade later they still languish in a career they despise. When they closed the casket or signed the divorce papers or sat down in their cubicle for what seemed like the millionth Monday, they couldn't help but feel slighted by the Almighty.

Days after returning, my disappointment morphed into a period of spiritual silence unlike any I'd known. I'd rise and prepare for my day each morning, brewing a pot of coffee and sitting in silence during the time I would normally pray. I'd start to speak, but words wouldn't come out. I didn't feel like I had much to say to a God who would allow these things to happen in the world He created, in the world He supposedly controlled. So I waited for God to say something only to find He was as quiet as I. Days swelled into weeks, but the God I'd committed my life to remained as scarce as mosquito thumbs.

Though never to this degree, I've experienced the absence of God before. I woke feeling as if God moved in the middle of the night without leaving a forwarding address. Or I got red-faced over something He did or didn't do, and I pushed Him away. Or we didn't have a falling-out; we just drifted apart. What am I to make of those moments when the One I long for has become *Deus absconditus*—the hidden God?[1]

When I can't hear God's voice, I often assume that He has left me. *Perhaps He is too busy, what with managing the world and all.* I fail to consider that maybe God *appears* silent because I've not been listening. Or perhaps He seems absent because I have stopped looking. Maybe that blurry figure in the distance is God waving me closer toward Him. Perhaps the muffled rumble is God whispering, "Here I am."[2]

After all, when I talk about the absence of God, I don't mean God no longer inhabits the space where I am. Some Christians have a conception of God up in heaven but coming to earth on occasion to visit mortals. This is not the Christian God, who is always present and available. By "absence," I am merely recognizing that I connect with God through relationship.

Absence is what I call those moments when God seems distant, when I feel disconnected from Him, when I find it difficult to communicate with Him. Absence describes the periods of spiritual darkness or spiritual silence when God seems to have left me.

In a culture that romanticizes romance, it is natural to think of relationships as forever honeymoons. I imagine the way two people's heads spin and hearts pound every time they see each other. But those who've been in long-term relationships know this is only a partial story. The other part is a deliberate act of hard work laced with moments of stress and strain and confusion, filled with muck and hubbub. In an earthly relationship, I can be mere inches from someone I love and yet feel miles away. And in my divine relationship, I'm learning to also expect ups and downs, highs and lows, periods of both closeness and distance, even as I fall more deeply in love with God.

•   •   •

The absence of God can be even worse for me as an evangelical Christian because we so rarely feel free to share our messiness with others in the Church. In an effort to look like I have it all together, I can easily hop in my car each Sunday with my game face on. I can greet everyone with honey sweetness and an ivory grin. As the music plays, I can lift up my hands, close my eyes, and sway ever so slightly back and forth. During the sermon, I can take copious notes and throw in an affirmative *mmmm-hmmmm* every now and again. But when I return home sometime later that afternoon, I've spent hours doling out a carefully crafted product in the presence of my spiritual brothers and sisters and yet shared so little of who I am.

As I share life with others, I realize that I'm not the only one putting on airs. Usually everyone else is too. As an old saying goes, "We tend to compare our insides with other people's outsides." So I take courage knowing I'm not alone in this struggle and every God follower is coming out of, entering into, or weathering a spiritual storm right now.

When Mother Teresa's letters were published in 2007, they shocked the world. People couldn't believe one of the greatest Christian icons of the last hundred years lived much of her life doubting, wrestling, struggling to understand God's ways and even more astonished that she often felt separated from God. She described her spiritual state as "torture" and her soul as an "ice block."

"Jesus has a very special love for you," Teresa wrote in a letter to a spiritual confidant, Michael Van Der Peet. "As for me, the silence and the emptiness is so great that I look and do not see, listen and do not hear."[3]

Maybe Mother Teresa should have seen this "spiritual dryness" coming. After all, her namesake was Saint Thérèse of Lisieux, who "lived most of her adult life in utter darkness and dryness and abandonment by her divine love."[4] Or perhaps she could have reflected on Saint John of the Cross, who coined the term "dark night of the soul" in the sixteenth century. As it turns out, even saints experience seasons of spiritual silence.

In the midst of Teresa's struggle, one of her spiritual mentors offered her three truths she needed.[5] In my period of divine absence, I wish I had them as well.

The first is that there is no human remedy for moments of spiritual darkness and silence. I may try to convince myself that if only I pray a smidge harder or volunteer more or spend a few more minutes reading the Bible, then I'll come through to the other side. But no silver bullet exists to slay it, and I must not feel responsible for affecting it.

It's also essential to know that the "feeling" of God's nearness is not the evidence of His presence. Jesus said fruit, not feeling, is the mark of faith. But for me, faith is wrapped up in emotion. So when I don't feel God, I assume something is broken and needs to be repaired. But the seeming absence of God is not like a noisy motor in the car you kept two years too long. Instead, it's like a fingerprint on a foggy window, a mark of something that once pressed against the pane and one day might press it again.

The feeling of absence is pain caused by the memory of presence. Absence is the condemned apartment building where you lived and laughed as a child. Absence is the half-empty bed that was once filled by a former spouse. Absence is the empty chair where your now-deceased husband used to sit and curse at a televised baseball game. The hurt felt in absence is a reminder that presence once existed in that place of pain. As Teresa's mentor said, craving God is evidence that God is already at work in our lives—a "sure sign" of God's "hidden presence."

Finally, God's absence can serve a purpose. Perhaps the greatest example of this truth is the gospel recounting of Good Friday, where we find Christ hanging on the cross and His weeping mother on her knees with a mouth too dry to speak. The Lord languishes for hours in the agony of God's absence—"My God, My God, why have You forsaken me?"

When the end comes, Jesus dies alone. The One who spent early mornings in the Father's presence, who was confirmed by God's voice at His baptism, dies in the shadow of God's absence. While I will never experience exactly what Christ did in that moment, I fear facing similar circumstances.

Jesus is better than I imagined because He understands my anguish in those moments when I beg God to provide a way out and God stares at me mum. Christ demonstrates what it looks like to cling to God when it feels like God has turned His back on me, and He teaches me that a sense of divine absence can be a waypoint on the road to redemption.[6]

God doesn't want to play a cosmic game of hide-and-seek. He wants to grow me, stretch me, and teach me. When I accept that God's quietude may mean He's up to something, it frees me to embrace rather than resist the experience. And when I open my hands to the mystery of divine absence, I'm challenged to start moving forward in faith again. Could it be that His seeming absence is not a scourge, but a gift?

After hearing these three truths, Mother Teresa thanked her mentor: "I can't express in words—the gratitude I owe you for your kindness to me—for the first time in…years—I have come to love the darkness."[7] Can I also come to embrace these times of darkness in my life?

Like Mother Teresa, the prophet Habakkuk experienced a shadowy night of his soul. "How long, Lord, must I call for help, but You do not listen?" he asks.[8] Again God seems to ignore him, at least at first. But this doesn't stop the prophet from seeking God. In the first chapter of the book bearing his name, Habakkuk asks God eight questions. And then he stands at the city ramparts and enters a standoff with God, refusing to move until God speaks.

We have no idea how long the prophet held his position, but I imagine it was more than a minute or two. Perhaps for days, he maintained his post, shifting weight from leg to leg while his eyes searched the skies for movement. When travelers passed by, they may have dropped a coin in his hat, thinking he was a crazy vagrant. Then God's voice shatters the stillness. He answers most of the questions the prophet posed—not often in the way Habakkuk would have wished—with a directness that shudders the spine.

After the last word falls from the Almighty's lips, Habakkuk tells us what the experience has taught him in the now-famous prayer:

> I heard and my heart pounded, my lips quivered at the
>   sound;
> decay crept into my bones, and my legs trembled.
> Yet I will wait patiently for the day of calamity to come
>   on the nation invading us.

Though the fig tree does not bud and there are no grapes
  on the vines,
though the olive crop fails and the fields produce no
  food,
though there are no sheep in the pen and no cattle in the
  stalls,
yet I will rejoice in the Lord,
I will be joyful in God my Savior.[9]

This dramatic story teaches me that though God may be hushed and hidden, He has not left for good. If I keep seeking and searching and speaking, God will return once more.[10] So I do not grow weary in my pursuits of the hidden One.

But Habakkuk also reinforces that God uses these times in my life to imbue me with good things I might not otherwise receive. As with the prophet, experiencing divine absence teaches me to trust when my spiritual spigot runs dry. "Will you follow Me even though you don't feel Me?" Jesus asks me in these moments. These periods are a gymnasium of faith where I develop my spiritual muscles so that I can rejoice in God even when He cannot be seen, felt, heard, or triangulated. They are the places where I come to believe that God is sovereign over death and life, darkness and light, noisiness and silence.

* * *

I'll never forget the moment after returning from Nepal when God's voice once again bridged the gap between us. I sat at my kitchen table with both hands wrapping a warm coffee mug. My study Bible and a stack of commentaries lay atop a computer that I was avoiding turning on.

As I had done many days before, I was stewing over my griev-
ances with God. I saw the eyes of those children in my mind—
big, brown, innocent eyes. I saw the smiles on their faces that
baffled me to no end. I visualized their home, their tableless
home, where they gathered every evening to worship a God who
didn't seem to be helping them out as much as He could. Once
again my heart filled with pity.

I looked around the room to take stock of all I had: a full refrig-
erator, two tables, and room to spare. Stacks of books and Bibles
and commentaries. *I have everything I need—much more than
I need.*

Then a most repulsive phrase welled up inside of me: *Maybe* they
should pity you.

These children had few of the things I was steeped in and they
wanted little. Their home was filled with joy and love and
vibrant, ongoing worship. They had no need for the items in
my possession, but I would give anything for what they had in
abundance.

God, I realize that life is not always as it seems, I said in my
heart. *I don't understand why life shakes out the way it does. I
can't wrap my mind around it all. But I trust You're still there
and still sovereign. And even if the stars fall like pearls from
a broken necklace, even if You never speak another word, I'll
keep trusting and following You.*

When I look back, this was the breaking point in my period of
divine absence. I felt God draw close. I started sensing His presence and nudges again. God never left. He was just giving me

some space. God isn't the annoying dad who pecks at you when what you really need is to be left alone. He knows that sometimes you need to experience His absence to crave His presence, and sometimes we know Him better by missing Him. In the moments when we only have fingerprints on a window, we learn to trust until His hand returns.

And it will.

10

Easter Remembrances

Encountering Jesus in Church

Christian community is not an ideal we have to realize, but rather a reality created by God in Christ in which we may participate.

—DIETRICH BONHOEFFER

More than a year had passed since the feeling of emptiness assaulted me after a church service and I'd prayed for God to show up and surprise me. So many God-moments since then, but at the time, I'd wondered whether the whole church thing was really worth it.

Today, the Easter sun punched through the clouds while I sat motionless in my church parking lot. The idling car hummed, and I tapped the steering wheel contemplating how the day might turn out.

The pastel-laden holiday has always been my fourth favorite of the year—after Christmas and Thanksgiving and my birthday, of course—and it still is. As a child, I'd wake to a surprise basket of candy left by an Easter Bunny that my parents made sure I knew didn't exist. After all, we didn't want to rob Jesus of the credit He deserved.

Mom would dress us boys because Dad had long left for church. At about nine o'clock the garage door would lift and we'd waddle out the door like ducklings. For several years, I donned seersucker overalls until my mother passed them down to my younger brother. I felt bad he got shafted with the getup, but my polyester suit with starched white shirt and clip-on paisley tie was hardly an improvement. Even still, something was always special about Easter for me as a child, and something was special about this one too.

I think of the growing number of my peers who've been disappointed by their churches, or perhaps injured by them. Their questions weren't answered or maybe they never felt permission to ask them. The church had proved so out of date that it had become one of many options for their spiritual growth, a formality or extracurricular activity that isn't necessary. The social benefits that church provides can be had elsewhere, and many thought they could do just fine on their own. They didn't need a church to pray or volunteer or study the Bible. Besides, any money invested in the church was largely used for institutional survival while the rest of the world languished from poverty, war, and disease. At best, they were disinterested; at worst, disillusioned and distrustful.

Over the years, many of my friends have walked away from the church, and the news headlines seemed to prove they'd made a wise choice. Televangelists embezzled from well-intentioned donors trying to sow "financial seeds" into God's kingdom, megachurch pastors cheated on their wives with their assistants, and priests molested their parishioners' children. People hadn't lost their faith, just their faith in church.

This has created several modern trends, not the least of which is a growing religious demographic labeled the "spiritual but not religious."[1] They are one of the fastest-growing religious segments and have helped make the "unaffiliated" the second-largest religious group in the United States. Most of them still pray and believe in God but they don't feel loyal to a local community of any kind.

Others still have tried to find a creative solution to the tension between their desire to connect with other believers and their disillusionment with the church. They've joined the increasing number of "Internet churches" or "Internet campuses" that are part of brick-and-mortar churches.

It has been said that communities can grow anywhere that communication occurs, and as electronic communication has bloomed, electronic communities have sprouted. From Facebook and Google+ to Twitter and LinkedIn, new community-oriented sites emerge almost daily, attracting millions. Devotees can log on at their convenience from anywhere with a connection and move on the minute they get bored.

Online churches operate on a similar platform. Once you join, you are usually given a login name and password that provides access to the site's ecclesiological products at any moment, day or night. Though each site offers its own operating system and unique services, they share in common the convenient access to a Christian community.

The most basic offering from an online church is a worship service. One online church I know of, for example, offers an electronic chapel with worship and prayer three times each day and additional services on special occasions. On Tuesday nights, it holds an "open house" with text-based teaching from a guest speaker.

Those sites associated with a physical church campus often just stream their services, but if you plan to attend one Internet campus I came across, make sure to come early because in the lobby area someone may invite you to "sit in their row." When this happens, chat tools allow you to converse during the service much like you would if you were physically next to each other.

These expressions of church are growing in popularity because of their unique ability to offer some of the benefits of church while eliminating some of the drawbacks.

Despite the emptiness inside me, I still caught glimmers of God in my physical church. I didn't want to leave it, and I wasn't comfortable in an online church. The church is a gathering of individuals who, when you are nearing the end of your rope, will tie it to a rock so you don't fly away. It is an otherworldly community where hurting people can enter and receive what Anne Lamott calls "spiritual chemotherapy," a powerful healing medicine that can hurt nearly as much as it helps. There is something supernatural about a bunch of angular people committed to living alongside one another, carrying one another's burdens and propping each other up when the world weighs us down.

I knew that spiritual fulfillment wasn't waiting in a cynical wasteland of religious criticism and freewheeling spiritual pursuits. While the prospect of a self-styled faith seemed attractive, after further reflection, I could not walk away from church. I didn't know the way forward, but I knew I loved God and that God loved the church. So much so that He gave His life for her.[2] If God died for her, I felt like I should find a way to live with her.

* * *

First Corinthians 6:19 is one of the most famous verses in the New Testament. It's also one of the most misunderstood.

"Do you not know that your bodies are temples of the Holy Spirit, who is in you, whom you have received from God?" Paul writes. "You are not your own."[3]

Growing up, I thought this passage was often quoted as reasoning for why I shouldn't drink myself silly or stuff my face with candy bars. While those are inadvisable actions, they are not exactly what Paul is addressing. The potential misunderstanding is due to a shortcoming in the English language. Unlike Biblical Greek, which can differentiate between the plural and singular forms of "you," English just gives us the one word and we're left to guess which is the case here. Unfortunately, some culturally conservative Christians have guessed wrongly. In the Greek, the "you" is plural and the "temple" is singular.

"Paul is saying, 'All of you *together* are a singular temple for the Holy Spirit,'" write E. Randolph Richards and Brandon J. O'Brien in *Misreading Scriptures with Western Eyes*. "God doesn't have billions of temples scattered around. Together we make the dwelling for the Spirit."

If I accept the popular mistranslation, Richards and O'Brien note, it might lead me to conclude, "I need to quit smoking." But once I do my homework, the application is that faith communities should behave and operate in ways that would please God as His *gathered* temple. This doesn't mean that my body doesn't matter or that God doesn't care about which behaviors I engage in. Rather, it tells me that God is calling me into a different kind of existence where I strive for holiness within the context of community. Paul is saying, as I've heard some put it, that while in the Old Testament, God had a temple for His people; in the New Testament, God has a people for His temple.

I cannot expect to experience Jesus fully or in the way He intended on my own. And, according to Scripture, I should strive for a relationship with the church that is both permanent and personal. That's why two of the primary metaphors for the church in the Bible are the Body of Christ (permanent) and the Bride of Christ (personal).

No part of a body can survive if separated from the whole. Worse still, cutting it off will cause it to cease to function as intended. Some Christians choose to be a lopped-off arm or severed leg, but I didn't want to miss out on the life that flows from being conjoined with others in community.

When Christians gather together, they become a temple. Holy. Hallowed. God shows up in some mysterious way. In the sacraments and songs, in the preaching and praying, in our commonality and differences. If I attempt to follow Jesus alone, I put my finger in the dike of God's presence waiting to flood my life. Like stones stuck together with divine mortar, something happens when I gather with others that can't happen any other way in any other place. I can learn how to pray and worship and serve and be a better friend. Being a part of a faith community forces me to coexist with people I didn't choose, to follow a God I can't prove. And in that space, I grow.

The church is often called the Bride of Christ in the Scriptures, and God has proven a long-suffering husband. His love remains strong—even when Christians don't live up to our names or we misrepresent Him or commit atrocities in His name. If I love God, I should at least try to love what He loves. Attempting to have communion with God and not His bride would be an act of cosmic divorce, to separate what God has put together.[4] Unlike me, Jesus isn't flighty and fickle. He is better than I imagined because He sticks with me—with all of us—for the long haul.

. . .

Talking about sticking with a faith community is far easier than actually *doing* it. The church is made up of people, and as a result, it is messy and difficult. People disappoint, fail, and hurt.

More than a decade ago, my father decided to plant a church. It wasn't an easy decision, but he was sure God was in it. When we left the congregation we'd served for nearly twenty years, some people got nasty. They fed rumors and avoided eye contact when we ran into them at the grocery store. This hurt deeply, and our family was forced to choose either to be bitter or to stay focused on what we believed God called us to. As a pastor's kid since birth, I know that faith communities can be as painful as they are grace-filled. Sticking with it isn't easy.

My friend Chris Heuertz has spent his life building communities around the globe. He says incompatibility is one of the communal struggles that is actually an "unexpected gift." When first formed, chemistry draws people into the community and keeps them there. But as time goes on and new people join us, chemistry changes. We have a choice to run or stay.

"If we want to be in true community, we have to make the choice to not give in to what's easy but instead to explore the unique gifts each person brings...often it's those who share the least amount of natural chemistry who work the best together," Heuertz writes. "It's in these relationships where we are sometimes most able to see beyond ourselves to the larger picture and bigger vision that unites us. These relationships become an illustration of true community. But they are not easy."[5]

I often silently assume that everyone in the church should be as perfect as the God they claim to serve. I think about a friend of mine who found out that two of the other members in her small group had cheated on their spouses with each other. She hadn't been a Christian long and felt burned, not just by her friends, but by God. She left the church and never returned. I often wonder what she might have learned if she had stayed. Maybe she would have learned how to forgive, how to suffer, how to love better. Now we'll never know.

* * *

At the same time, I can't expect the church to be my spiritual everything. As I look back on the emptiness that once visited me, I realize that I had placed unrealistic expectations on the church. I'd been relying on it to fill me up and keep me full, to be the primary if not the only place I encountered Christ. As I learned to experience Jesus on a regular basis in my life, I was better able to experience Jesus in a local faith community. I'd forgotten that church was not a landing place but a launching pad. Not a finish line but a starting block. I had made the church my single source of spiritual vitality. But the church is not the source but a conduit.

During my spiritual quest, I still attended church most weekends when I was in town, but only physically. Emotionally, I left myself on that chair where I begged God to invade my life. For months, a shell of me had shown up smiling each Sunday, but today was different. I knew it was time to drop the pose and reengage. I was ready.

I can't tell you what songs were sung that day or whom I sat next to. I don't recall how long the service ran or if any babies cried during the preaching. But I remember that I felt Jesus's presence there. In the handshakes and baptisms and even the plastic thimble of grape juice with vacuum-sealed wafer. New life was all around me—Denise with her hair back at its normal length, Carl carrying his heart pump and smiling, and a young girl in a sunflower dress in the chair where Hannah used to sit.

I've now realized that these signs of God's presence have always been there, but I'm now open to them. I've let go of the unfair expectations I'd placed on a community whose shoulders were not designed to bear such a weight. And through it all, I've realized that the key to revitalizing my faith was learning to experience God in the everyday and the all the time, not just during Sunday gatherings.

In order to experience Jesus in His fullness, to see Him as He is and not as I had imagined Him, I have to keep searching for Him in the unlikely gifts I receive each day. And this includes the place I most expected to find Him: the mysterious community of faith.

+

A Prophecy in 13B

All who call on God in true faith, earnestly from the heart, will certainly be heard, and will receive what they have asked and desired, although not in the hour or in the measure, or the very thing which they ask. Yet they will obtain something greater and more glorious than they had dared to ask.

—MARTIN LUTHER

The winter wind whipped as my plane descended into Boston's Logan Airport. Remnants of December's snow remained in shadowy places, and the chill pressed in on the cabin windows. I was en route to Rockport, Massachusetts—a town famous for pretending to be Sitka, Alaska, in *The Proposal* starring Sandra Bullock—where I was teaching a writer's workshop.

For three days, I spent time with aspiring writers sharing tips and tricks I'd learned about the industry during my short but intense career. I gave the final talk on storytelling and the power of narrative to inspire readers and open their minds to new ways of thinking. After the talk concluded and I was packing my bag, three women standing near the exit approached me.

"We have a word from God for you," one of them said as I turned to approach them.

I froze but maintained a cautious smile.

The women explained that they were friends who had met at a church with a long name that had the word "revelatory" in it. It sounded like the kind of place that calls its pastor "apostle" and lets people dance during the sermon. As a Southern Baptist, I've always been skeptical of these kinds of Christian experiences.

"Can we pray over and anoint you?" one asked.

Not wanting to be rude, I agreed.

I walked back into the room and sat in a chair while these women encircled me. One pulled a vial of oil from her purse and anointed my forehead while a second instructed her to rub it on the bottoms of my shoes as well.

"'Beautiful are the feet of those who carry the good news,'" she whispered, quoting from the prophet Isaiah and Paul's letter to the Romans.

The women then laid their hands on my neck and shoulders, praying and offering a word of knowledge. For twenty minutes I sat in a conference room chair in pseudo-Sitka being prayed over, but I barely heard a word any of them spoke. I was busy thinking about what I'd eat for lunch and how weird this whole experience was and whether or not that oil would give me forehead acne. When they finished, they said they'd e-mail me everything they'd seen and heard in case I missed anything. I thanked them and left.

Later, I shared the story with some friends, poking fun at the whole experience and explaining how "you can't make this stuff up." I had just placed my carry-on bag in the overhead bin on my return flight when I felt my phone buzz in my pocket. One of the ladies had sent me the e-mail she'd promised. She attached an audio file they recorded during the experience, but she said she felt compelled to type a particular portion out so I wouldn't miss it. As I read the message she claimed God had given her, my hands trembled:

Expect the unexpected. Look for the unusual. Get out of the box because things are shifting. Things are changing.

Life as you know it will not be the same. For I am changing things. Places that you have been in for a long time—places that feel like they aren't going to change—are shifting. There is an opening to a new place.

You have thought this a difficult season—this situation would not change. In fact, you have gotten comfortable in a strange way with this trial. A comfort that has caused complacency. But I am stirring you up. Stirring you up to greater things. Shake off the past. The door is open before you. Stand up and walk through it.

I grew unaware of the line of passengers shuffling down the aisle beside me, and sank deep into seat 13B. *Who told them that I've been writhing through one of my life's most difficult seasons or that I've grown complacent in the midst of it? And how could they know that I have been journeying in search of an "unexpected God"?*

I wept the entire flight home.

The word from those ladies was a punctuation mark on a year in which life seemed to be conspiring to take me to a new place in my spiritual journey. When I returned home, I listened to the entire recording. They described how God was working in my life with precision, but I could not get the words she typed in the e-mail out of my mind: "But I am stirring you up."

A prophetic utterance. A promise. An invitation to continue my pilgrimage.

Months earlier I'd begun reaching to touch God's face, to see and experience God in new ways. I'd prayed for God to show up in my life, and He'd answered my pleas. I found moments of respite and enlightenment in the Scriptures, no longer read out of duty. My eyes caught surprising glimpses of God in far-off monasteries and my back porch. I saw Jesus flash in the eyes of orphans and the touches of refugees. In chance meetings with unlikely angels in unusual places, I stumbled across the One I craved. Now I realize He was there all along. He had just been waiting for an invitation to meet me on His terms, rather than mine.

The search for our boundless God has no beginning and no end. When we walk through one door of spiritual awakening, God opens another and beckons us to come. He calls us not to a destination but to a lifelong posture whereby we live aware, peering around every corner knowing that God may be waiting there.

I think of Simeon, the devout old codger who believed the Holy Spirit had promised him he wouldn't die before he saw the Messiah. I imagine when the doctor told him he had rheumatoid arthritis and a heart murmur, Simeon probably wondered if he'd heard God correctly. After all, his hearing had been failing lately. But a few moments later, he'd shake off his doubts and start looking again.

Every time Simeon heard the growl of an approaching caravan or news of a traveler passing through town, adrenaline would flood his veins. *Maybe today will be the day I'll peer into the eyes of Israel's Chosen One.* When Simeon first glimpsed the young Christ child, he was overwhelmed with joy, swept the baby up in his arms, and blessed God.

Simeon had learned what too many Christians—myself included—have forgotten. To live with wide eyes. Expectant.

Scanning horizons and peeking around corners, looking for God in the unlikely places and faces. *Maybe today will be the day.*

As I pursue Jesus, I want to engage my ears, not just my eyes. "See that you do not ignore the Voice that speaks," the author of Hebrews writes.[1]

The Voice, whether It shouts or whispers, never ceases. It comes in the still moments when I stop talking and listen instead. When I'm sharing the secret parts of myself with God and those I love. When I'm in the holiest of sanctuaries as well as the sacrilegious spaces I think God couldn't possibly inhabit. In the chaos of the workday and the middle of the night, shaking me from my slumber. The Voice speaks through prayers and prophetic utterances and when I'm reading a familiar Scripture passage and a fresh phrase jumps off the page.[2]

The Voice is speaking, of that I am sure.

But are you listening, looking, and expectant?

The living God is waiting, and He is better than you imagined.

Notes

0 | Holy Expectation

1 1 Corinthians 12:27
2 See Mark 6:52.
3 John 3:8
4 Jeremiah 33:3, MSG

1 | Christ in the Desert

1 They take the Bible literally, and David says, "Seven times a day I praise you." (Ps 118:164) They pray once at night—"at midnight I praise you" (Ps 118:62)—and at dawn.
2 *Rule of Saint Benedict*, chapter 43.
3 1 Thess 5:17 c.f. Luke 18:1
4 "Your very silence shows you agree," Euripides once said. God has said he can be trusted, that he will speak. And silence demonstrates that we agree.
5 Kathleen Norris describes the same observation in her book *The Cloister Walk*: "Gladly, my perspective on time has changed. In our culture, time may seem like an enemy: it chews up and spits out with appalling ease. But the monastic perspective welcomes time as a gift from God, and seeks to put it to good use rather than allowing us to be used up by it." (p. xix)
6 Luke 1:13–15a
7 See Luke 5:15–16. c.f. Mark 1:35.
8 Isaiah 30:15
9 Zechariah 2:13
10 Some fled the new invention called Christianity, which was little more than a state-blessed religion perpetuated by Emperor Constantine. This pseudo-Christianity promised status and prosperity rather than self-giving sacrifice. "[The Desert Fathers] exposed the underside of a

form of religion that fuels our hunger for self-centered living," noted Bradley Nassif in *Christianity Today.*

11 It is important to note that they did not abandon gospel proclamation or evangelism. They didn't turn inward. In Syria, for example, Saint Simeon preached from a forty-foot column and converted many Bedouins to Christ (see Bradley Nassif in *Christianity Today).*

12 *Reaching Out,* pp. 37–38.

2 | And a Mighty Wind Blows

1 Psalm 150: 16a
2 Job 12:7
3 See Stephen Shoemaker, *Godstories,* p. 128.
4 Psalm 139:7–12
5 Stephen Shoemaker, *Godstories,* p. 133.
6 Tozer, *Knowledge of the Holy*

3 | Cereal Snowflakes

1 These descriptions are referenced from, respectively, Romans 11:33 NIV, Romans 11:33 ESV, Romans 11:33 HCSB, Romans 11:33 NASB, Psalm 147:5 NRSV, Psalm 147:5 NASB, Psalm 147:5 NKJV, Psalm 147:5 NLT, Job 37:23 MSG, Job 36:26 NIV, Job 36:26 NIV, Job 36:26 HCSB, 1 Kings 8:12 NIV, 1 Timothy 6:16 NIV.

2 Isaiah 40:13, NIV 1984
3 *The Soul of Kierkegaard: Selections from His Journals*
4 A phrase borrowed from Rudolph Otto in *The Idea of the Holy.*
5 For more discussion on this, see Steven Boyer and Christopher A. Hall, *The Mystery of God: Theology for Knowing the Unknowable,* pp. 15–16. "If we say that the sun is 'invisible,' we mean not that it is unavailable to our vision but that it overpowers our vision; not that it cannot be seen but that it cannot steadfastly be looked," they write.

6 See Boyer and Hall, *The Mystery of God,* p. 5.
7 See Barbara Brown Taylor, *Bread of Angels.*
8 Exodus 16:31
9 1 Corinthians 4:1
10 1 Corinthians 1:18; c.f. 1 Corinthians 4:10, where Paul writes, "We are fools for Christ..."
11 See *Jesus Manifesto,* p. 88.

4 | Mountains beyond Mountains

1 "Suffering," *The New Yorker,* George Packer, January 25, 2010 (http://www.newyorker.com/talk/comment/2010/01/25/100125taco_talk_packer).

2 To learn more about their work, check out www.hopeinternational .com, or Peter's book *The Poor Will Be Glad: Joining the Revolution to Lift the World Out of Poverty*.

3 "Haiti's Angry God," *The New York Times*, Pooja Bhatia, January 13, 2010 (http://www.nytimes.com/2010/01/14/opinion/14bhatia .html?_r=0).

4 Luke 1:37, NLT

5 Jeremiah 32:17

6 James 4:2

7 c.f. Luke 4:14–28; Mark 6:1–6, NIV

8 Mark 6:6

9 Luke 4:30

10 Matthew 18:3, NIV

11 James Whitehead, "The Religious Imagination," *Liturgy 5* (1985), 54–59. C.S. Lewis also touched on this idea when he said, "Reason is the natural order of truth, but imagination is the organ of meaning." Lewis believed that humans want to be more than themselves and in order to do this, they demand windows. For this reason, Lewis often commented that he lived "almost entirely in [his] imagination." His mind's eye became the core of his being and millions of people have conceived of God in fresh ways as a result. (See also Ephesians 3:20.)

12 I was first introduced to the idea of looking twice by Barbara Brown Taylor in *The Preaching Life*, pp. 47–52.

13 Matthew 13:13–15

14 E. B. White, *Essays of E.B. White* (New York: HarperCollins, 1977), p. 8. I first discovered this essay in the introduction to Brennan Manning's *All Is Grace*.

5 | A Thread Called Grace

1 Jonathan Merritt, "An Evangelical's Plea: 'Love the Sinner,'" *USA Today*, April 20, 2009 (http://usatoday30.usatoday.com/printedition/news/20090420/column20_st.art.htm).

2 Ibid.

3 Genesis 3:10 (VOICE)

4 Parker Palmer, *A Hidden Wholeness*, p. 4.

5 Frederick Buechner, *Wishful Thinking: A Seeker's ABC* (New York: HarperOne), p. 106.

6 "When we honestly ask ourselves which person in our lives means the most to us," Henri Nouwen wrote, "we often find that it is those who, instead of giving advice, solutions, or cures, have chosen rather to share our pain and touch our wounds with a warm and tender hand."

7 Genesis 17:1

8 Exodus 3:14, 15b

9 John 8:58

10 John 14:27

11 See Frederick Buechner, *Wishful Thinking: A Seeker's ABC*, p. 83.

12 "What does the word Shalom mean?" (http://www.hillel.org/about/news/2010/aug/27aug10_shalom.htm).

13 Brené Brown, *I Thought it Was Just Me*, p. xxv.

6 | Dying to Live

1 See Genesis 5.

2 Genesis 6:8–9

3 Genesis 7:6

4 As opposed to Frederick Buechner's commentary on Noah: "If God needed a rainbow as a reminder, [Noah] thought, that could mean that if someday God didn't happen to look in the right direction or had something else on his mind, he might forget his promise and the heavy drops would start pattering down on the roof a second time." (*Peculiar Treasures,* pp. 138–139.)

5 Psalm 62:1

6 Isaiah 40:31

7 James 1:12

8 Acts 1:4, NIV—emphasis added.

9 During the editing phase of this book, Carl was bumped to the A-list and admitted to the hospital, where he expects to wait three to six months for a new heart.

10 NIV

11 Jeremiah 17:5–8

7 | The Last Lullaby

1 James 2:23

2 See John 15:15.

3 John 10:4, NIV

4 See "Flock and Awe," *The Sydney Morning Herald,* July 25, 2012; "Sheep may be dumb…but they are not stupid," *The Guardian,* March 5, 2005; "Sheep not so stupid after all, scientists say," *Toronto Sun,* February 22, 2011.

5 Barbara Brown Taylor, *Teaching Sermons on Suffering: God in Pain,* p. 126.

6 See Barbara Brown Taylor, *Gospel Medicine,* p. 21.

8 | Revelation at the Ping-Pong Emporium

1 Christiane Lauterbach, "The Unorthodox Church of Grant Henry," *Atlanta,* April 2011 (http://www.atlantamagazine.com/dining/articles/2011/4/1/discovery-sister-louisas-church1/print).

2 It's important to note that "religion" can be a good thing when it sees faith in God as an end and not a means and when it is outwardly and upwardly focused rather than inwardly focused (see James 1:27). Which is to say, when it is not "religion" as we know it at all.

3 James 1:27, NLT

4 Paraphrased

5 The prophet Amos channels the same divine frustration at the Israelites' empty religiosity when he writes the following in Amos 5:21–24:

> I hate, I despise your religious festivals; your assemblies are a stench to me. Even though you bring me burnt offerings and grain offerings, I will not accept them. Though you bring choice fellowship offerings, I will have no regard for them. Away with the noise of your songs! I will not listen to the music of your harps. But let justice roll on like a river, righteousness like a never-failing stream!

6 Luke 15:11–32, paraphrased

7 For more on the difference between religion and true faith rooted in the Gospel, see Tim Keller, "The Difference Between Religion and the Gospel" (http://theresurgence.com/2012/01/18/the-difference -between-religion-and-the-gospel).

8 Not coincidentally, Mark includes the curse of the fig tree in the same passage where he records Jesus clearing the temple courts, another affront to the religious establishment.

9 "Christianity is a relationship with Jesus the Christ. When things go wrong, it's not because we don't understand certain doctrines or fail to follow particular commands. It's because we have lost our 'first love,'" Leonard Sweet and Frank Viola write in *Jesus Manifesto*, pp. 39–40.

10 Reinhold Neibuhr, *An Interpretation of Christian Ethics*, pp. 138–139.

11 See Taylor, *Home by Another Way*, p. 34.

12 See Barbara Brown Taylor, *Home by Another Way*, p. 144.

13 See the imagery of the torn veil in Matthew 27:51.

14 Eugene Peterson, *The Jesus Way: A Conversation On The Ways That Jesus Is The Way*, p. 211.

9 | A Tableless Home

1 See Isaiah 45:15.

2 See Barbara Brown Taylor, *Gospel Medicine*, pp. 74–75.

3 David Van Biema, "Mother Teresa's Crisis of Faith," *TIME*, August 23, 2007.

4 As quoted by John Ortberg, "When God Seems Far Away," for *Leadership Journal* (October 2011).

5 David Van Biema, "Mother Teresa's Crisis of Faith," *TIME*, August 23, 2007.

6 I first read of these first lessons in John Ortberg's article "When God Seems Far Away," for *Leadership Journal* (October 2011). See also Barbara Brown Taylor, *Teaching Sermons on Suffering: God in Pain*, pp. 112–113.

7 David Van Biema, "Mother Teresa's Crisis of Faith," *TIME*, August 23, 2007.

8 Habakkuk 1:2, NIV

9 Habakkuk 3:16–18, NIV

10 Jeremiah 33:3, James 4:8

10 | Easter Remembrances

1 According to some polls, one-third or more of young Americans consider themselves "spiritual but not religious."

2 Eph. 5:25

3 NIV

4 "Jesus Christ cannot be separated from His church. While Jesus is distinct from His Bride, He is not separate from her. She is, in fact, His very own body in the earth." *Jesus Manifesto*, p. 141.

5 Heuertz, *Unexpected Gifts*, pp. 145–146.

+ | A Prophecy in 13B

1 Hebrews 12:25, paraphrased

2 Barbara Brown Taylor also reflects on this idea in *Mixed Blessings*, pp. 23–24.

Acknowledgments

When I decided to become a writer, I thought the key to success would be talent. A decade of years and hundreds of thousands of words later, I realize that this is secondary. The road to any success we may accomplish must be paved by God and sojourned with friends. For this reason, I would like to thank the following people:

To my family, you are an enduring source of strength in my life. And you stick by me even when it would be easier to fall away.

To the entire FaithWords team, who has now given me three opportunities to publish. Working with you is a writer's dream. Specifically, I want to thank Jana Burson, my friend first and editor second. Thank you for believing in me and pushing me. Adrienne Ingrum, whose insight honed this manuscript beyond what I was able to do myself. And Shanon Stowe, the best publicist any author could ask for.

To Margaret Feinberg, my friend and mentor, to whom this book is dedicated. Your integrity, work ethic, commitment to excellence, and love for God inspire me.

To Chris Ferebee, my literary agent and friend. You're a rock of comfort and a well of industry knowledge. I look forward to many more years working alongside you.

I want to thank the enduring and encouraging friends who've helped me believe in myself when I questioned my ability and calling: Ken Coleman, Brad Lomenick, Rebekah and Gabe Lyons, Bob Goff, Leif Oines, Will Franz, Ed Stetzer, Marty Duren, Kirsten Powers, Jason Locy, Tyler and Natalie Wigg-Stevenson, and Carolyn Haggard.

To those who read early drafts and provided critical feedback: Lindsie Yancey, Scot McKnight, Savana Southerland, Karen Swallow Prior, Rachel Held Evans, Sarah Baik, Chris Stedman, Maegan Carberry, Ryan Reid, Mandy Anderson, and Jamie Smith.

To Barbara Brown Taylor, whose sermons and insights challenged me to look deeper into the Bible as I searched for God's fingerprints in this world.

To all of my editors, particularly Kevin Eckstrom, Stephanie Smith, David Graham, John Wilson, Yonat Shimron, Roxanne Wieman, Garance Franke-Ruta, Elizabeth Tenety, Eric Marrapodi, and Glen Nishimura.

And because the last turns out to be first, thank you to Abba for refusing to walk away from me even when I gave you every reason to run. You sustain me when I am tempted to collapse under the weight of my imperfections.

To all I have forgotten, grace and gratitude.

About the Author

Jonathan Merritt is a faith and culture writer who has published more than one thousand articles in outlets such as *The Atlantic*, *USA Today*, *National Journal*, the *Washington Post*, and CNN .com. He is senior columnist for Religion News Service, America's largest provider of news and commentary focused on religion and spirituality. His previous books include *A Faith of Our Own: Following Jesus Beyond the Culture Wars* and *Green Like God*, which *Publishers Weekly* called "mandatory reading for churchgoers."

Recently named one of thirty leaders reshaping Christian leadership by *Outreach Magazine*, Jonathan has become a popular speaker at conferences, colleges, and churches. As a respected Christian voice, he has been interviewed by *ABC World News*, Fox News, CNN, NPR, PBS, Politico, Slate, and the *New York Times*.

Jonathan sits on the national board of directors for Bethany Christian Services, America's largest adoption and orphan care agency. He holds master's degrees from Southeastern Baptist Theological Seminary and Emory University's Candler School of Theology.

Follow Jonathan on Twitter: @jonathanmerritt.